a taste
of PESACH

Perhaps you can put them together as one volume?

A PROJECT OF
YESHIVA ME'ON HATORAH (ROOSEVELT)

TO BE ADDED TO OUR MAILING LIST
FOR FUTURE RECIPE SAMPLERS:

email atasteofpesach@gmail.com

call 845-352-1270

fax 845-352-7217

mail P.O. Box 428 / Monsey, NY 10952

PUBLISHED BY **ARTSCROLL / SHAAR PRESS**

313 REGINA AVENUE / RAHWAY, NJ 07065 / (718) 921-9000
WWW.ARTSCROLL.COM

DISTRIBUTED IN ISRAEL BY **SIFRIATI / A. GITLER**

MOSHAV MAGSHIMIM / ISRAEL

DISTRIBUTED IN EUROPE BY **LEHMANNS**

UNIT E, VIKING BUSINESS PARK, ROLLING MILL ROAD
JARROW, TYNE AND WEAR, NE32 3DP / ENGLAND

DISTRIBUTED IN AUSTRALIA AND NEW ZEALAND BY **GOLDS WORLD OF JUDAICA**

3-13 WILLIAM STREET / BALACLAVA, MELBOURNE 3183, VICTORIA / AUSTRALIA

DISTRIBUTED IN SOUTH AFRICA BY **KOLLEL BOOKSHOP**

NORTHFIELD CENTRE / 17 NORTHFIELD AVENUE / GLENHAZEL 2192 / JOHANNESBURG, SOUTH AFRICA

ISBN-10: 1-4226-1472-7 / ISBN-13: 978-1-4226-1472-3

PRINTED IN PRC

I find that I end up using your recipes year round because they're tasty, practical & they work!!

When I started making my own פסח last year, I asked my friends and family for some tried and true recipes. All the good recipes that I got were the 'Roosevelt Recipes'. Thank you...

...you did it again! ...delicious recipes! ...easy to follow!!

Every פסח, at the סדר, my grandchildren say to me, "Bubby, this is really delicious. Did you get the recipe from the Roosevelt cookbook?" Invariably, they are right!

The majority of my pesach menu comes from my collection of your cookbooks!

I actually tried almost all of them. My family & friends loved & enjoyed them all.

The notes you see throughout the book are feedback we've gotten over the last six years. We hope you enjoy reading them as much as we enjoyed receiving them!

It's been seven years since we first sat down around

a kitchen table to plan a Pesach recipe sampler as a fundraiser for Yeshiva Me'on HaTorah (Roosevelt). By now, tens of thousands of households across America and beyond have enjoyed our recipes. We've been gratified by the warm reception and the outpouring of positive responses. For a while now, many of you have been asking us to consolidate the pamphlets into a user-friendly book — and so we are pleased to offer you *A Taste of Pesach*.

Looking back, we've been trying to figure out what has made our recipe samplers so successful. We think that we have the answer.

While we enjoy working together, we are a pretty diverse group.

Among us are working mothers who need quick and easy recipes and stay-at-home-mothers who have more leisure time for cooking. Some of us are super-organized and prepare everything in advance; others do everything at the last minute. For a few of us, it's all about cooking large quantities quickly; for others, exquisite individual presentations are a priority. Some of us cook on a budget; others will splurge on more exotic items. Some of us serve only healthful foods; others enjoy serving an indulgent treat, especially for Yom Tov.

Yet, while there is a lot that makes us different, there is so much more that makes us the same.

We all want to enhance Pesach with food that will get rave reviews from family and guests. We want user-friendly, visually attractive recipes, with accurate cooking times and yields. We want to see what the food that we are making will really look like when we're done. We want recipes that have broad appeal and that work. We're just like you.

With so many cooks represented, there is something here for everyone. We've compiled a blend of traditional recipes that have been used for generations and modern, up-to-date recipes. From gefilte fish to sushi-style tuna, you are sure to find recipes that appeal to you and all the members of your family, no matter what your style is. The clear and precise instructions make it easy to try new recipes, so you can feel comfortable experimenting with something different. Best of all, you can be sure that all the recipes were triple-tested in our kitchens — which look very much like your kitchens — so that every recipe will come out perfect, every time.

With so much work going into Pesach, we hope that our cookbook will make your menu choices and food preparation that much easier. Enjoy!

From our hearts to yours,

Reva Bess, Gitty Eisenberg, Raizy Greisman, Goldy Joseph, Hindy Langer, and Fraidi Neiman on behalf of Yeshiva Me'on HaTorah (Roosevelt)

חנה Thank you so much for the Pesach recipe books! We enjoy many of the recipes on Pesach and throughout the year!

TABLE OF CONTENTS

WE ALL ENJOYED THEM ON PESACH, AND CONTINUE TO DO SO ALL YEAR ROUND!

Thank you so much for the very useful + delicious cookbooks! I'd been saving them over the years + finally put them to good use this year when I started cooking for פסח!

Love, love, love the cookbooks!

I especially appreciate you sending me 3 previous books since all of mine were flooded in Sandy!

Each recipe is a gem! Keep them coming!

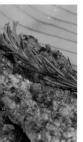

MENU

Appetizer

Traditional Gefilte Fish, *82*

Beet Salad, *66*
Carrot Salad, *66*
Russian Cole Slaw, *70*

Cream of Chicken Soup, *34*

Entrée

Soft and Savory French Roast, *132*
Onion Chicken, *108*
Potato Kugel, *140*
Apple Strawberry Crisp, *150*
Skewered Vegetables, *138*

Dessert

Fruity Compote, *184*
Toll House Bars, *203*

appetizer

Seared Tuna, *78*

Fried Sweet Potato Salad, *62*

entrée

Lamb Chops, *118*

Whipped Potatoes with Basil, *158*

Vegetable Julienne, *134*

dessert

Strawberry "Short-cut," *192*

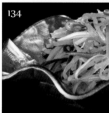

IDEAS

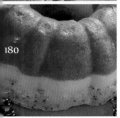

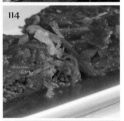
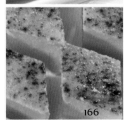

THANK YOU

Rabbi Meir Zlotowitz and Rabbi Gedaliah Zlotowitz

For giving us the opportunity and pleasure of working with you and the ArtScroll team:

Mrs. Felice Eisner, Devorah Bloch, Eli Kroen, Mrs. Judi Dick, Mrs. Goldy Helfgott, and Mrs. Tova Ovits

Your professionalism and attention to detail are evident on every page.

Our VERY understanding and supportive

Husbands and Families
including our Fabulous Kid Taste-Testers

Eliyahu, Levi, Tzvi Menachem, Shimshon Zelig, Mordechai L., Nosson, Sara Ettel, Devorah Leah, Adina, Chaim, Penina, Chedva, Nechama E., Ephraim, Basya, Elisheva, Mordechai E., Rosi, Rivky, Shlomo Zalman, Leeba, Tzipora, Henny, Aharon, Nechama B., Sara, Shimshy, Chava Leah, Reuvain, Moishy, Yossi, Chaya, Mechi G., Anshel, Peri, Malky G., Chavi, Mechy N., Malky N., Shaya, Moshe, Zecharya

THANK YOU FOR SHARING YOUR FAVORITE RECIPES AND FOR LENDING YOUR TABLEWARE FOR THE PHOTOGRAPHS

Etty Akerman, Idy Appel, Chani Bandman, Dina Bernath, Rochie Bernfeld, Mrs. Carol Bess, Chaya Bienenstock, Mrs. Hindy Birnbaum, Estee Bixenspanner, Mrs. Gitta Bixenspanner, Debbie Brody, Mindy Chesir, Mrs. Goldie Dubin, Dream Cabinetry, Chani Ehrman, Chani Eichorn, Chanie Eichorn, Bracha Eidelman, Rivky Eisenberg, Rebbetzin Shlomis Eisenberg, Mrs. Etty Ellenbogen, Shani Ellenbogen, Diane Epstein, Brochie Feifer, Nechama Feigenbaum, Rochel Feller, Esther Rochel Fischer, Rivky Fishman, Rochel Fishman, Dina Frank, Malky Frankel, Chaya Freidman, Layala Fruchter, Esty Galinsky, Rivky Gelman, Malky Glatt, Chani Goldberger, Malky Gordon, Rachel Grey, Mrs. Toby Griesman, Sara Gutwirth, Mrs. Rivky Halberstadt, Rivky Halpern, Mrs. Shatzy Heller, Chana Esther Hertz, Mrs. Chani Hertz, Mindy Hirsch, Etty Hirsh, Yael Hoffman, Nechama Holtz, Mrs. Miriam Ilowitz, Mindy Joseph, Miriam Joseph, Miriam Kahn, Gitty Kerpel, Rivky Kleiman, Ayala Klein, Blumie Klein, Surivky Klein, Chevy Kramer, Mrs. Rivky Krasnow, Mrs. Rochelle Langer, Laya Lapides, Bruriah Lebowitz, Chumie Levitan, Gitty Lipshitz, Mrs. Sarah Lowy, Mrs. Henie Meisels, Malkie Meisels, Mrs. Bleemie Mushell, Chayitty Neiman, Mrs. Nechama Neiman, Ariella Neuberger, Mrs. Pearl Neuhauser, Batsheva Newhouse, Baila Parnes, Chani Piller, Preva Pollack, Shuli Prager, Mrs. Beth Rabinowitz, Chumie Rosenbaum, Brana Rosenblum, Frumie Rosengarten, Pessy Rothschild, Miriam Sauer, Gayil Schwab, Ruchie Schwab, Tami Schwab, Bassi Silber, Bracha Skolnick, Mrs. Toby Spiegel, Mrs. Faiga Malka Stefansky, Mrs. Faigy Stein, Chani Steinfeld, Shani Steinfeld, Ayala Sternheim, Sara Gitty Strauss, Mrs. Chaya Swerdloff, Nechama Taub, Shani Taub, Rivky Tenenbaum, Leah Tress, Mr. Joel Ungar, Tzina Ungar, Naomi Weinberger, Mrs. Rochel Weiss (Digestive Wellness), Zahara Weiss, Esther Wolkenfeld, Chani Zahler, Ariella Zicherman, Mrs. Raizy Zicherman

WITH GRATITUDE TO HASHEM FOR GIVING US THE PRIVILEGE OF PRODUCING THIS BOOK TO BENEFIT YESHIVA ME'ON HATORAH.

PHOTOGRAPHY David Ticktin   DESIGN Raizy Greisman

CLASSIC SWEETBREADS

MEAT . YIELDS 6 SERVINGS

2   pounds sweetbreads

1   Tablespoon vinegar

4   Tablespoons oil

2   large onions, diced

1   red pepper,
    cut into thin strips

2   stalks celery, diced

1   cup fresh mushrooms,
    sliced

2½ Tablespoons potato starch

2   cups chicken soup OR
    reserve 2 cups sweetbreads
    cooking liquid

1   teaspoon salt

⅛   teaspoon pepper

Note: *Sweetbreads should be cooked as soon as possible after purchasing, as they do not store well.*

1   Place sweetbreads into a 6-quart pot with vinegar. Add water to cover. Bring to a boil; reduce heat to simmer. Cook sweetbreads for 45 minutes, or until soft.

2   Drain (If using cooking liquid, reserve 2 cups before draining) and immediately plunge sweetbreads into cold water to stop the cooking process. Carefully remove and discard membranes and tubes. Cut sweetbreads into 1-inch pieces.

3   In a deep skillet or pot, heat oil and sauté onions, red pepper, celery, and mushrooms until tender, 15-18 minutes.

4   Dissolve potato starch in 1 cup chicken soup or reserved cooking liquid, stirring until smooth. Add to pot; slowly stir in remaining chicken soup or reserved liquid. Add salt and pepper. Cook for 3 minutes until thickened.

5   Add sweetbreads and cook for additional 2 minutes.

To create a perfectly squared mound of mashed potatoes for the base of your sweetbreads (or any other appetizer), center a square cookie cutter on a plate and spoon in mashed potatoes until it is tightly packed. Carefully lift off cookie cutter.

I roasted cherry tomatoes to serve with this appetizer and loved the combination. Beads of two sauces (I used dill dip, page 80, and thick tomato sauce) pressed from a squeeze bottle complete the look.

Another idea is to serve the stack in a pool of warm (store-bought) marinara sauce. A little quicker and easier, but just as tasty!

EGGPLANT STACK

PAREVE . YIELDS 8 SERVINGS

2   eggs

¼   cup seltzer

½   cup potato starch

1   teaspoon salt

1   large OR 2 small eggplants, not peeled

    oil for frying

    sauces, optional, for serving

1 **Prepare the batter:** Beat first four ingredients in a bowl, using a fork or hand mixer.

2 Scrub eggplant and slice into rounds.

3 Heat 2 tablespoons oil in a large skillet. Dip each eggplant slice into batter and fry for 2-3 minutes on each side until golden, crispy on outside and soft inside. Add more oil as needed.

4 Stack 3 or 4 slices and serve with sauce, if desired.

Yom Tov calls for many heavy dishes at each meal. This fruit cup is a pleasantly light way to start a seudah. To cut down on preparation time, use two 16-ounce cans of pineapple tidbits instead of fresh pineapple.

GOURMET FRUIT

PAREVE . YIELDS 15 (1-CUP) SERVINGS

1   box strawberry gel dessert

    arils of 3 pomegranates

1   fresh pineapple

1   (11-ounce) can mandarin oranges, drained

6   kiwis, diced

2   mangoes, diced

SAUCE

½   cup raspberry syrup (such as Kedem)

6   Tablespoons sugar

½   cup orange juice

2   teaspoons fruit or nut liquor

1   Prepare gel dessert according to package instructions. Allow to jell.

2   Cut the pineapple into chunks; place into food processor fitted with the S-blade. Pulse on low until pieces are small, but not crushed. Drain liquid.

3   Combine all fresh and canned fruit and mix gently to combine. Drain as much liquid as possible. Add 1 cup of prepared gel dessert (save the rest for your kids!). Toss gently.

4   Combine sauce ingredients. Pour over fruits.

CHICKEN-WRAPPED ASPARAGUS SPEARS

MEAT . YIELDS 6-8 APPETIZER SERVINGS

4 boneless, skinless chicken breasts, thin sliced or pounded thin, cut into ¼-inch strips

1 pound asparagus spears, tough part of stems cut off

MARINADE

3 Tablespoons olive oil

4 Tablespoons lemon juice

4 minced garlic cloves or frozen cubes

salt, to taste

pepper, to taste

1 **Prepare marinade:** Combine oil, lemon juice, garlic, and seasoning in a large ziplock bag; add chicken. Let marinate at least 2 hours in the refrigerator.

2 Preheat oven to 350°F. Lightly grease a baking sheet or line with parchment paper.

3 Remove chicken from marinade; discard marinade. Wrap each chicken strip in a spiral around an asparagus spear; secure the ends with toothpicks. Place on prepared baking sheet.

4 Bake 20-25 minutes, until chicken is done. Do not over-bake or asparagus will darken and wilt and chicken will dry out. Remove toothpicks before serving.

If you're looking for something that will plate beautifully without too much effort, you must try these. My twelve-year-old daughter, Chaya, prepared them for the photo shoot — if she can do it, you can too.

We used white asparagus because it does not need to be checked for insects. If you use green asparagus, the colors will contrast better, making for a prettier presentation. Please note that green asparagus must be checked properly.

These hush puppies scream "KIDS!!!!" To create the "corkscrew hot dog" pictured, start at the end of a hot dog, cutting about halfway through with a sharp knife held on an angle. Holding the knife steady, rotate the hot dog so that it is cut at that angle all the way down. Heat in the oven at 425°F for 30-45 minutes, until it opens and looks done.

HUSH PUPPIES

MEAT . YIELDS 32 HUSH PUPPIES

6	large potatoes
3	Tablespoons oil
2	large onions, diced
	salt, to taste
	pepper, to taste
8	hot dogs
½	cup Pesach crumbs

DIPPING SAUCE

1¼	cups ketchup
1	cup vinegar
¼	cup apple juice
¼	cup brown sugar
¼	cup honey
⅓	cup oil
3	cloves garlic, minced
2	teaspoons salt
	pepper to taste

1 Peel potatoes and cut into chunks.

2 Heat oil in medium saucepan over low heat. Add diced onions to oil, spreading so they cover bottom of pan. Add potatoes. Cover and cook over low heat for 25-30 minutes, stirring occasionally, until onions are golden brown and potatoes are easily pierced with a fork.

3 Remove from heat. Add salt and pepper; mash well.

4 Preheat oven to 350°F. Line a baking sheet with parchment paper and spray lightly with nonstick cooking spray.

5 Cut hot dogs into quarters. Coat each quarter with about 2 tablespoons mashed potato mixture. Roll in Pesach crumbs. Thread hush puppies onto skewers, if desired. Place on prepared baking sheet.

6 Bake for 30 minutes. Serve warm with dipping sauce.

7 **Prepare dipping sauce:** Combine all sauce ingredients in a medium saucepan.

8 Cook over medium heat, stirring occasionally until small bubbles form. Remove from heat.

Stop trying to mimic your chometz-coated-schnitzel taste! This is an all-around favorite for adults and kids alike. Great for a Yom Tov meal or a Chol HaMoed supper. Best when served fresh.

POTATO KUGEL-CRUSTED SCHNITZEL

MEAT . YIELDS 8 SERVINGS

1½ cups ground almonds, divided

2 eggs

¼ cup seltzer

4 potatoes, finely grated and drained

salt, to taste

pepper, to taste

oil for frying

1 pound chicken fingers or boneless chicken breasts cut into strips

1 Prepare three bowls:
   BOWL 1: 1 cup ground almonds
   BOWL 2: 2 eggs beaten with ¼ cup seltzer
   BOWL 3: grated potatoes combined with ½ cup ground almonds, salt, and pepper.

2 Prepare oil in a deep skillet for frying by placing it over medium-high heat. In order for potato kugel batter to stick to the chicken, make sure that the oil is very hot.

3 While oil is heating, dredge chicken cutlets in **BOWL 1**, dip into **BOWL 2**, then coat with mixture in **BOWL 3**.

4 Fry 5-7 minutes on each side.

About 10 minutes into a taste-a-thon in the bungalow colony, I came across a large empty bowl. I turned to my friend Chaya and asked what I had missed. She showed me this salad on her plate and told me to take a taste. It was out of this world, and I saw why it was the first salad to be finished to the bottom of the bowl. Thank you, Rochel, for this great recipe!

SALMON SALAD

PAREVE . YIELDS 6 SERVINGS

4   (6-ounce) salmon fillets

1   Tablespoon olive oil

½   teaspoon salt

¼   teaspoon pepper

1   teaspoon dried oregano

1   teaspoon dried basil

1   head Romaine lettuce, shredded

1   avocado, cubed

1   red onion, thinly sliced

DRESSING

⅓   cup vinegar

¼   cup oil

⅓   cup sugar

¾   teaspoon pepper

1   **Prepare the fish: Up to one day in advance, preheat oven to 450°F. Place salmon fillets onto a preheated grill pan. Drizzle with olive oil and sprinkle with spices and herbs. Grill for about 20 minutes. Chill until ready to serve.**

2   **When ready to serve, prepare the salad: On each plate, mound lettuce; sprinkle with avocado and red onion. Remove skin from salmon fillets and crumble fish over center of mound.**

3   **Place dressing ingredients into a small jar and shake vigorously to combine. Divide between salad portions.**

Serve with your favorite mushroom sauce or the pictured onion medley purée: Dice one small onion, one leek, three scallions, and two shallots. Sauté in two Tablespoons olive oil until translucent. Do not allow to brown. Add salt and pepper to taste. Use an immersion blender to purée. Serve at room temperature.

TWO-TONE MEATLOAF

MEAT . YIELDS 20 SERVINGS

MEAT FILLING

2	Tablespoons oil
1	large onion, diced
1½	pounds ground meat
1	egg, beaten
1	teaspoon salt
¼	teaspoon pepper

CHICKEN FILLING

1½	pounds ground chicken
1	onion, grated
2	Tablespoons barbecue sauce or ketchup
1	egg, beaten
½	teaspoon salt
¼	teaspoon pepper
½	teaspoon garlic powder

1 In a skillet, heat oil and sauté onion until translucent. Let cool and combine with remaining meat filling ingredients.

2 In a separate bowl, combine chicken filling ingredients.

3 Line a 9 x 13" pan with parchment paper. Flatten meat mixture evenly to cover most of paper. Shape chicken filling into a log and center it vertically over the meat mixture. One at a time, fold sides of meat mixture over chicken mixture, using the parchment paper to help you. Alternately, you can flatten chicken mixture over meat and roll up jelly roll style. (If the mixtures are too soft to work with after spreading on parchment paper, freeze for 1-2 hours, until firm.)

4 Place meatloaf into freezer for 4 hours. When firm, remove from freezer and slice into one-inch slices. Place slices on a parchment paper-lined baking sheet.

5 Preheat oven to 350°F. Bake, uncovered, for 25-30 minutes.

While having dinner at an exclusive restaurant, I ordered a very elegant-sounding appetizer. When it came to the table I was delighted with the pleasant blending of everyday flavors to create a gourmet dish. I was even more delighted when I realized how simple this would be to recreate at home!

TROPICAL AVOCADO

PAREVE . YIELDS 6 SERVINGS

12 Portobello mushroom caps

olive oil

salt, to taste

2 ripe avocados

1 (8-ounce) bag baby spinach leaves

2 cups fresh or frozen strawberries, quartered

2 ripe mangoes, cubed

1 can hearts of palm, cut into small pieces

freshly ground black pepper

Clean and check all salad ingredients.

1 Preheat oven to 450°F.

2 Spray a baking sheet lightly with nonstick cooking spray. Place cleaned mushroom caps, gill side up, onto sheet. Drizzle with olive oil and sprinkle with salt and pepper.

3 Roast for 25 minutes, or until tender.

4 When ready to serve, remove avocado flesh from shell and mash well.

5 Gently mix with spinach leaves, strawberries, mango cubes, and hearts of palm to combine.

6 Use a small container, such as a half-pound deli container, to mold. Invert onto plate and gently shake to unmold. Sprinkle with freshly ground black pepper.

7 To serve, place 2 grilled mushroom caps next to molded salad on each plate.

I was skeptical about trying this recipe because it seemed almost too simple. Well, it proved to be simply delicious — even my kids will agree with that.

For a bit of a different look and a heartier, more meaty feel, I ask at the deli counter to have the pastrami cut into one-inch cubes.

GLAZED PASTRAMI

MEAT . YIELDS 6 SERVINGS

1 Tablespoon oil

1 onion, diced

2 (8-ounce) cans tomato sauce

3 Tablespoons water

4 Tablespoons sugar

2 Tablespoons honey

1 pound pastrami slices

1 In a medium pot, heat oil. Add onions and sauté until soft.

2 Add tomato sauce, water, sugar, and honey. Bring to a boil, stirring to combine.

3 Add pastrami and reduce heat. Simmer for 30 minutes.

To plate as pictured, serve over a bed of mashed potatoes.

My favorite recipe in this year's book was the Glazed Pastrami.

The pastrami appetizer was a big hit.

LONDON BROIL SALAD

MEAT . YIELDS 8 SERVINGS

1 (2-pound) London broil

MARINADE
½ cup dry red wine

½ cup oil

2 cloves garlic

3 Tablespoons lemon juice

⅛ teaspoon pepper

¼ teaspoon onion powder

SALAD
1 head Romaine lettuce, shredded

2 plum tomatoes, diced

½ red onion, thinly sliced

½ cup toasted slivered almonds (optional)

original Terra chips, coarsely crushed

DRESSING
⅓ cup vinegar

¾ cup sugar

¾ cup oil

1 teaspoon imitation mustard

1 teaspoon salt

1 Combine marinade ingredients and place into a large ziplock bag; add London broil. Marinate at least 3 hours or overnight in the refrigerator. Remove meat from marinade; discard marinade. Place meat into a roasting pan.

2 Preheat oven to high broil. Broil for 10-12 minutes on each side. Allow to cool and slice thinly against the grain. Store covered in refrigerator until ready to use. Bring to room temperature before serving.

3 **Prepare the dressing:** Place dressing ingredients into a cruet or jar. Shake vigorously to blend ingredients thoroughly.

4 In a large bowl, toss lettuce, tomatoes, and onion. Mound salad in the center of 8 appetizer/salad plates. Arrange London broil slices over mound. Drizzle with dressing and sprinkle with almonds and Terra chips.

london broil salad is your the best we've ever tasted.

SOUP

When deciding who would be the first to test this recipe, I jumped at the chance. My daughter doesn't eat carrots, so I am always on the lookout for soup ideas sans carrots. She only agreed to taste this after I vouched that there were no carrots in it despite the carrot-y color. She loved it.

RED PEPPER-SQUASH SOUP

PAREVE . YIELDS 8 SERVINGS

2 medium onions

2 medium zucchini with peel

2 large red peppers, seeds removed

2 Tablespoons oil

1 Tablespoon chicken consommé powder (optional)

salt, to taste

pepper, to taste

1 Cut onions into quarters. Cut squash into large chunks (peel on). Cut peppers into chunks about the same size as the squash.

2 Heat oil in a large pot. Add onions, squash, and peppers. Do **not** add water. Cover and cook over low heat for 1½-2 hours, stirring occasionally. Add chicken consommé powder, if using, and salt and pepper to taste. Stir to combine.

3 Blend with an immersion blender.

A great recipe that may look like a "regular" vegetable soup, but is in fact much tastier and heartier. A satisfying soup that hits the spot when everyone troops in "starving" after a long Chol HaMoed outing. So simple to make, as most of the vegetables are shredded in the food processor, and it freezes well.

HEARTY SHREDDED VEGGIE SOUP

MEAT . YIELDS 8 SERVINGS

⅓ cup oil

3 medium onions, diced

1 leek, white and light green parts only, thinly sliced

1 bunch celery, diced

2 strips boneless flanken

1½ pounds carrots, shredded

2 small zucchini, shredded

1 yellow squash, shredded

salt, to taste

pepper, to taste

1 Heat oil in an 8-quart pot over medium-high heat. Add onions, leek, and celery and sauté until soft. Add the meat and brown on each side for about 5 minutes.

2 Add all the shredded vegetables in the following order, cooking for a few minutes between additions: carrots, zucchini, squash.

3 Cook for 30-45 minutes, stirring occasionally. Add salt and pepper to taste. Add water to cover, plus two cups. Lower heat to medium-low and simmer for 2 hours.

WHITE VELVET SOUP
WITH HONEYED CHESTNUT GARNISH

MEAT/PAREVE . YIELDS 12 SERVINGS

2	Tablespoons olive oil
2	large leeks, white and light green parts only, chopped
4	medium parsnips, peeled and cubed
½	turnip, peeled and cubed
4	white potatoes, peeled and cubed
2	stalks celery, sliced
6	cups chicken soup OR water
1	cup coffee whitener
3	teaspoons salt
¼	teaspoon white pepper

HONEYED CHESTNUTS

10	roasted chestnuts (from bag)
1	Tablespoon margarine
2	Tablespoons honey

1 **Prepare the honeyed chestnuts:** Slice chestnuts thinly. Combine margarine and honey in small saucepan; bring to a boil over medium heat. Add sliced chestnuts and cook until golden, 5-7 minutes.

2 **Prepare the soup:** Heat oil in an 8-quart soup pot. Add leeks and sauté over low heat for 5 minutes, or until softened. Add parsnips, turnip, potatoes, and celery. Continue sautéing over medium heat, stirring frequently, for several minutes.

3 Add chicken soup or water. Bring to a boil; simmer, covered, for 15-20 minutes over medium heat. Vegetables should be soft enough to pierce with fork easily. Remove from heat.

4 Add coffee whitener, salt, and pepper and blend with immersion blender. Place over low heat; heat thoroughly.

5 To serve, ladle into individual bowls and garnish with honeyed chestnuts.

The honeyed chestnuts are a great garnish that can really be used for any thick soup. You might want to make extra because you will find yourself nibbling!

When seasoning the soup, make sure to use white pepper as listed so that you don't spoil the white velvety look with black specks.

For all of you who like to cook in advance, this is the soup for you. It freezes beautifully.

BUTTERNUT SQUASH SOUP

MEAT/PAREVE . YIELDS 8 SERVINGS

2 medium butternut squashes (4-5 pounds)

3 medium onions

4 Tablespoons oil

4 cloves garlic

6 cups chicken stock OR
6 cups water + 1 Tablespoon chicken consommé powder

salt, to taste

pepper, to taste

1 Preheat oven to 425°F. Line a baking sheet with parchment paper. Cut squashes in half vertically. Scoop out the seeds and discard. Place squash, cut sides down, onto prepared sheet. Bake for 40 minutes, or until soft. Remove squash from oven and scoop out the flesh.

2 Heat oil in a 6-quart pot over medium heat. Add onions and garlic and sauté until translucent.

3 Add scooped out squash flesh to pot. Add stock or water and seasonings. Bring to a boil; lower heat and simmer for 1 hour. Blend with an immersion blender.

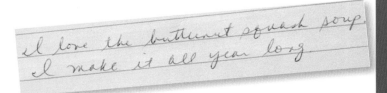

I love the butternut squash soup. I make it all year long

Every recipe in this book is tasted and triple-tested by the cookbook team. We loved the idea of a cream of chicken soup, but the first recipe we tried tasted too much like regular chicken soup. We went back to the drawing board and, if we may say so ourselves, this is a winner! Very much like chicken soup with a heartier, creamier feel.

CREAM OF CHICKEN SOUP

MEAT . YIELDS 10 SERVINGS

1   bunch celery

3   potatoes

2   Tablespoons oil

1   onion, diced

¾   pound chicken cutlets, sliced

7   cups chicken soup OR 7 cups water + chicken bones

salt, to taste

pepper, to taste

1   Cut celery into chunks. Peel potatoes and cut into cubes.

2   Heat oil in an 8-quart pot over medium heat. Add onion and sauté until soft. Add celery and continue to sauté for 3 minutes. Add sliced chicken and potatoes.

3   Add chicken soup, or alternatively, add 7 cups of water and chicken bones in a mesh bag. Add salt and pepper and bring to a boil; lower to a simmer and cook for 1½ hours. Remove bones, if used.

4   Blend soup to desired consistency.

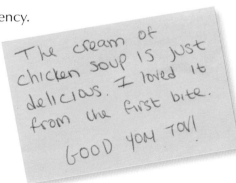
The cream of chicken soup is just delicious. I loved it from the first bite. GOOD YOM TOV!

Each Sunday when I sit down to make the weekly menu with my kids, this soup is always included. When putting together recipes for the cookbook, this zucchini-leek soup just had to make it, so we adapted the recipe for Pesach. I am sure it will be a winner with your kids, too.

ZUCCHINI-LEEK SOUP

PAREVE . YIELDS 8 SERVINGS

2 Tablespoons oil

1 onion, diced

1 leek, white and light green part only, sliced

4 large zucchini, peeled and cut into chunks

½ Tablespoon chicken consommé powder

1 Tablespoon onion soup mix

1 Tablespoon parsley flakes

salt, to taste

pepper, to taste

1 In a 6-quart pot, heat oil over medium-high heat. Add onion and sauté until translucent.

2 Add leek to pot. Sauté 7-10 minutes.

3 Add zucchini. Sauté an additional 7-10 minutes.

4 Add remaining ingredients, stirring until smooth. Add cold water to cover (about 4 cups). Bring to a boil and cook 1½ hours.

5 Using an immersion blender, blend soup, leaving enough texture so that the soup still has body.

The menfolk in my family cannot get enough of this soup. So hearty and filling — it's almost a meal on its own!

CABBAGE-BEEF SOUP

MEAT . YIELDS 20 SERVINGS

¼ cup oil

2 Spanish onions, diced

2 pounds flanken OR stew meat, cut into bite-size pieces

2 Tablespoons vinegar

1¼ cups brown sugar

¼ cup sugar

2 Tablespoons paprika

3 Tablespoons salt

½ Tablespoon pepper

2 (16—ounce) bags shredded green cabbage

3 large carrots, shredded

1 (15-ounce) can crushed tomatoes

1 Heat oil in a large stockpot set over medium heat. Add onions and sauté until translucent. Add meat and sauté until well browned, about 20 minutes.

2 Add vinegar, brown sugar and sugar and stir until well combined and meat is coated. Add paprika, salt, and pepper and cook additional 3-5 minutes to blend flavors, stirring often and scraping bottom of pot.

3 Add cabbage, carrots, and tomatoes; stir. Add water to cover plus 2 more inches up side of pot. Bring to a boil; reduce to a rapid simmer. Cook for 2 hours.

My cousin Rivky is a frequent "donor" to my recipe box. Whenever I call her she has something good to share. This is her favorite soup recipe. Not your typical mushroom soup, it is easy to prepare and freezes well.

Turn this into a cauliflower soup by substituting mushrooms with a 1-pound bag of frozen cauliflower and omitting the creamer.

ROASTED MUSHROOM SOUP

MEAT . YIELDS 8 SERVINGS

4	cloves garlic, crushed
4	Tablespoons olive oil
3	Portobello mushroom caps, cleaned and quartered
3	onions, quartered
5	cups chicken soup
2	Tablespoons white wine
	salt, to taste
	pepper, to taste
¾	cup nondairy creamer

1 Preheat oven to 425°F. Line a baking sheet with parchment paper.

2 In a small bowl, mix crushed garlic and olive oil. Place mushrooms and onions onto prepared baking sheet; drizzle with olive oil mixture. Roast for 45 minutes or until soft.

3 Transfer to a 6-quart stock pot and add chicken soup, wine, salt, and pepper. Bring to a boil; lower heat and simmer for 10 minutes. Cool slightly and blend with immersion blender.

4 Stir in creamer and bring to a boil again before serving.

As soon as we finished taking this photo, I ate the soup straight from the bowl, down to the bottom. (And I never thought I liked potato soup!) A wonderfully foolproof recipe, it comes out yummy every time.

POTATO SOUP

PAREVE . YIELDS 12 SERVINGS

3 Tablespoons oil

3 medium onions, diced

4 stalks celery, sliced

4 large carrots, sliced

1 parsnip, sliced, optional

2 Tablespoons potato starch

9 cups cold water, divided

8 potatoes, peeled and cut into chunks

3 Tablespoons salt

pepper, to taste

1 Heat oil in an 8-quart pot. Add onions, celery, carrots, and parsnip, if using. Cover and cook over low heat for 30 minutes to release liquids. Stir frequently, checking to make sure veggies are not burning.

2 When vegetables are soft, stir in potato starch and mix well. Add 1 cup cold water and mix well. Add remaining 8 cups water, potatoes, salt, and pepper and bring to a boil. Lower heat and cover pot. Cook, covered, until potatoes are soft, about 30 minutes.

3 If you would like a thicker consistency, mash some of the potatoes with a spoon against the side of the pot.

ASPARAGUS SOUP
WITH VEAL MINI-MEATBALLS

MEAT . YIELDS 12 SERVINGS

2 bunches asparagus

4 Tablespoons oil

4 onions, diced

2 Tablespoons salt

12 cups chicken stock

6 potatoes, cubed

VEAL MEATBALLS
¾ pound ground veal

1 clove garlic, minced

1 teaspoon parsley flakes

1 egg

2 Tablespoons potato starch

1 **Prepare the soup:** Cut off the asparagus heads and tough parts of the stem, and peel off the thorns. Cut asparagus into small pieces.

2 Heat oil in an 8-quart pot. Sauté onion in oil for 5 minutes until translucent. Add asparagus and sauté for 5 minutes. Add remaining ingredients and cook for 1½ hours, stirring occasionally. Purée with an immersion blender until smooth.

3 **Prepare veal meatballs:** Combine all meatball ingredients. Form into 1-inch mini-meatballs. Drop into puréed soup and cook for ½ hour.

The mini-meatballs in this soup are a great accompaniment that perfectly complements the asparagus flavor. When I tried this recipe at home to see if it should be included, my family rated it 10+!

To celebrate my mother-in-law's 60th birthday, we
hired Chef Chani Goldberger for an interactive
cooking demo. Due to her spunky personality
and delicious dishes, we all had a grand time. This
soup is one of her signature creations.

When pumpkin is not in season,
use butternut or Calabaza squash.

PUMPKIN SOUP

MEAT . YIELDS 8 SERVINGS

4 cups chicken stock

½ cup extra virgin olive oil

3 leeks, white part only,
cleaned and chopped coarsely

1½ pounds pumpkin, peeled,
seeded, and cut into chunks

1 cup dry white wine

salt

freshly ground black pepper

1 Heat chicken stock in a small saucepan.

2 Meanwhile, in a 6-quart stockpot, heat oil and sauté leeks until
soft and wilted, 6-7 minutes. They will shrink to about half their
original size.

3 Add pumpkin to stock pot. Stir and sauté additional 2 minutes.

4 Add wine. Cook 2 minutes. Add hot stock, stir, and partially
cover the pot. Bring to a boil. Add salt and pepper to taste.
Lower heat and simmer for 1 hour.

5 Cool slightly and purée with an immersion blender, leaving
some large chunks. Taste and adjust seasoning.

As a new kallah I went to my mother-in-law for Pesach. Upon arriving on Erev Pesach, I went into the kitchen to ask what I could help with. She set me up to make lukshen. After two crepes she looked at my thick, omelet-like crepes and sent me to take a shower!

PERFECT PESACH LUKSHEN

PAREVE . YIELDS 12-16 CREPES

Could you please include a no-fail lukshen recipe? I have so many versions + would love the "one" perfect one.

8	eggs
1	cup potato starch
1	cup water
½	teaspoon salt
	oil, for frying

1 Beat eggs lightly; add remaining ingredients. Don't overbeat.

2 Heat 1 tablespoon oil in a 10" nonstick frying pan. Pour a scant ¾ cup batter into hot pan and swirl to cover the bottom completely. As soon as batter is set, use a spatula to carefully flip over for 15 seconds. Remove from pan and continue until all batter is finished. You may need to regrease pan between crepes.

3 Roll a few crepes up at a time and slice thinly to make "lukshen."

BEET-LETTUCE SALAD

PAREVE . YIELDS 6-8 SERVINGS

BEETS

3 beets, unpeeled

1 cup vinegar

½ cup sugar

½ cup water

SALAD

1 (8-ounce) bag lettuce

1 red onion,
sliced into thin rings

1 avocado, diced

DRESSING

½ cup vinegar

½ cup olive oil

½ teaspoon salt

1 **Prepare the beets:** Preheat the oven to 350°F. Scrub unpeeled beets with a vegetable brush. Wrap in foil and bake for 1 hour, until soft. Combine vinegar, sugar, and water in a large container or ziplock bag. Peel whole beets and add to bag. Marinate overnight in the refrigerator.

2 **Prepare the salad:** In a large bowl, combine lettuce, onion, and avocado. Remove beets from marinade and cut into cubes. Add to salad. (I don't like to toss this salad at any stage before serving, because the beets will turn everything red.)

3 **Prepare the dressing:** In a small container, combine dressing ingredients. Pour over salad.

Pesach makes me think of beets. In my mind's eye I see my grandmother's hands stained red from peeling beets for her traditional borscht and homemade horseradish. While I must admit I don't serve either of those, this salad was a welcome walk into the past for me.

To avoid staining your hands, use disposable gloves when handling the beets.

CRUNCHY CABBAGE SALAD

PAREVE . YIELDS 8 SERVINGS

1 (8-ounce) bag red cabbage

1 (8-ounce) bag green cabbage

3 scallions, white part only, sliced

½ cup toasted slivered almonds

½ cup pomegranate arils OR dried cranberries

DRESSING

1 cup mayonnaise

¼ cup sugar

¼ cup vinegar

⅓ cup water

2 cloves garlic, crushed

⅛ teaspoon pepper

salt, to taste (about 1 teaspoon)

1 Place all salad ingredients into a large serving bowl.

2 **Prepare the dressing:** Combine dressing ingredients in a container and shake vigorously.

3 Pour over salad and toss right before serving so that salad stays crunchy.

Since I was introduced to this salad at the cookbook photo shoot, I must have made it 15 times for Kiddushim, tea parties, Shabbos seudahs, or "just because." Each time, I have been complimented on a great salad but my friendly requesters had to wait until now to get the recipe.

Shallots are really different from onions in taste and texture, so do not be tempted to substitute!

ROASTED SWEET POTATO SALAD

PAREVE . YIELDS 10-12 SERVINGS

1 large sweet potato, cut into thin strips

1 Tablespoon olive oil, plus more for drizzling

salt, to taste

pepper, to taste

garlic powder, to taste

2 shallots, sliced

2 (8-ounce) bags Romaine lettuce

¾ cup glazed pecans, crushed

DRESSING

¼ cup olive oil

¼ cup white wine vinegar

¼ cup sugar

4 garlic cloves, crushed

1 Preheat oven to 375°F. Line a baking sheet with parchment paper.

2 Place sweet potato strips in a single layer on prepared baking sheet. Drizzle with oil, salt, pepper, and garlic powder. Roast for 1 hour.

3 Sauté shallots in 1 tablespoon olive oil until browned and edges are crispy.

4 **Prepare the dressing:** Place dressing ingredients into a small container and shake to combine thoroughly.

5 In a large bowl, layer lettuce, sweet potato, and shallots. Pour dressing over and sprinkle with nuts right before serving.

"FLATBREAD" SALAD

PAREVE . YIELDS 12 SERVINGS

"FLATBREADS"

- 3 cups almond flour (see note on page 200)
- 1½ teaspoons kosher salt plus more for topping
- 2 eggs
- 2 Tablespoons olive oil

  dried minced onion

  dried minced garlic

DRESSING

- ½ cup oil
- ¼ cup vinegar
- ½ cup sugar
- 1 garlic clove OR frozen cube
- ½ teaspoon imitation mustard

  salt, to taste

  pepper, to taste

SALAD

- 2 (8-ounce) bags Romaine lettuce
- ½ (8-ounce) bag shredded red cabbage
- 15 grape tomatoes, halved
- 1 avocado, cubed
- 1 red onion

1 **Prepare "flatbreads":** Preheat oven to 350°F.

2 Knead together almond flour, 1½ teaspoons kosher salt, eggs, and olive oil to form a soft dough. Divide dough into 2 balls.

3 Use a rolling pin to flatten dough between 2 pieces of parchment paper on a cookie sheet until about ½-inch thick. Remove top layer of parchment paper. Cut dough into 2-inch squares. Sprinkle liberally with kosher salt, minced onion, and minced garlic.

4 Bake for 10 minutes or until golden brown.

5 **Prepare the dressing:** In a bowl or container, combine all dressing ingredients and whisk until blended.

6 Place salad ingredients into a large bowl. Toss with dressing. Top with "flatbreads" just before serving.

A great low-carb alternative to traditional potato salad.

UN-POTATO SALAD

PAREVE . YIELDS 6 SERVINGS

1 medium (about 3-pound) butternut squash peeled, seeded and cubed

1 small carrot, finely grated

2 sour pickles, finely diced

2½ Tablespoons sour pickle juice

⅛ teaspoon salt

¼ cup mayonnaise

1 Place squash cubes into a vegetable steamer over 2 inches water in a saucepan. Cover tightly and simmer until squash can be pierced with a fork, but is not mushy, approximately 15 minutes. DO NOT OVERCOOK. Drain squash.

2 Combine warm squash with carrots and pickles in a large bowl.

3 Place mayonnaise into a small bowl. Gradually add sour pickle juice, stirring to combine between additions. Add salt; stir until smooth. Pour over salad and gently toss to combine.

Although this salad is best served warm, it can be made in advance and stored in the refrigerator for 4-5 days.

When we taste-tested this salad, we all enjoyed it so much that we argued over who gets to take home the leftovers! (There were none. Argument over!) A twist on the classic broccoli salad, this gives you a satisfying crunch with a delicious mingling of tastes.

BROCCOLI STALK SALAD

PAREVE . YIELDS 8-10 SERVINGS

1	bunch fresh broccoli	**DRESSING**
4	carrots, sliced	
3	ounces toasted slivered almonds	½ cup mayonnaise
⅓	cup dried cranberries	⅛ cup vinegar
½	small red onion, diced	1 teaspoon salt
		2 Tablespoons sugar

1 Cut florets from broccoli stalks and discard, as they are often infested. Wash stalks well, or peel. Cut stalks into thin round discs. Peel carrots and slice into round discs.

2 Combine all salad ingredients in a bowl.

3 **Prepare the dressing:** In a small jar, combine dressing ingredients and shake well, or blend with an immersion blender.

4 Pour over salad and toss well.

Can be stored for 2-3 days in the refrigerator.

New and improved! Plain enough for those with
simple taste buds but still a welcome change.
This is one salad that is particularly pretty
served individually — even the rosy hue of the
dressing adds beauty!

GRILLED CHICKEN SALAD

MEAT . YIELDS 8-10 SERVINGS

1 pound skinless, boneless chicken breast halves	**DRESSING**
½ cup slivered toasted almonds	⅓ cup red wine vinegar
1 cup sliced strawberries (fresh or frozen)	½ cup sugar
	1 cup olive oil
1 (8-ounce) bag Romaine lettuce	½ onion, minced
	1 teaspoon salt
	¼ teaspoon ground white pepper

1 **Prepare the chicken:** Lightly oil a grill pan and place over high heat. When hot, add chicken. Grill chicken 8 minutes on each side, or until juices run clear. Alternately, broil in oven set to Broil High for 5 minutes on each side, or until done. Remove from heat, cool, and slice into strips.

2 **Prepare the dressing:** Place all dressing ingredients into a container. Using an immersion blender, process until smooth.

3 Arrange lettuce on serving plates. Top with grilled chicken slices, strawberries, and almonds. Drizzle with dressing to serve.

TOMATO-MUSHROOM SALAD

PAREVE . YIELDS 12 SERVINGS

8 plum tomatoes

1 (8-ounce) can mushrooms, drained

2 scallions, thinly sliced

DRESSING

½ cup oil

½ cup vinegar

6 Tablespoons sugar

3 teaspoons salt

2 cloves garlic, crushed

1 Slice tomatoes into rounds ¼-inch thick. Place into a serving bowl or container. Add mushrooms.

2 **Prepare the dressing:** Place all dressing ingredients into a container or cruet. Shake well or blend to combine.

3 Pour dressing over tomatoes and mushrooms. Add scallions and toss gently, or lay out as pictured and drizzle with dressing.

A great accompaniment to meat or fish, and it goes well with matzo too.

AVOCADO SALAD
WITH PORTOBELLO MUSHROOMS

PAREVE . YIELDS 10 SERVINGS

5   Portobello mushroom caps

olive oil, for drizzling

salt, to taste

pepper, to taste

3   kirbies OR small cucumbers

2   ripe avocados, peeled and cubed

1   pint grape tomatoes, halved

¼   cup toasted pine nuts

DRESSING

¼   cup olive oil

1   clove garlic, crushed

1   Tablespoon lemon juice

½   teaspoon oregano

½   teaspoon basil

½   teaspoon salt

1   Preheat oven to 425°F. Line a baking sheet with parchment paper.

2   Clean mushroom caps and remove gills. Place mushroom caps on prepared pan, gill side up. Drizzle with olive oil and sprinkle with salt and pepper. Roast for 10-15 minutes, or until edges begin to brown. Remove from oven and slice.

3   **Prepare the dressing:** Place dressing ingredients into a cruet or jar. Shake to blend thoroughly.

4   Peel kirbies and cut in half lengthwise. Cut each half into thin half-moons. Combine with avocados, tomatoes, mushrooms, and pine nuts in a large bowl.

5   Pour dressing over salad and toss gently.

SWEET POTATO CRISPS SALAD

PAREVE . YIELDS 8 SERVINGS

1 large sweet potato

¾ cup oil for frying

SALAD

1 (8-ounce) bag Romaine lettuce

½ red pepper, sliced into strips

½ yellow pepper, sliced into strips

1 (8-ounce) can hearts of palm, drained

1 small red onion, diced

DRESSING

½ cup olive oil

⅓ cup vinegar

½ cup sugar

3 cloves garlic, crushed

1 teaspoon imitation mustard

1 **Prepare sweet potato crisps:** Peel sweet potato. Using a vegetable peeler, continue to peel wide paper-thin strips of sweet potato.

2 Heat oil in a deep skillet. When oil is hot, add sweet potato strips a few at a time. When golden and crispy (about 5-7 minutes) remove with a slotted spoon. Can be made a few days in advance; store in an airtight container at room temperature.

3 **Prepare the dressing:** Place dressing ingredients in a small container. Shake to combine.

4 **Assemble salad:** Combine salad ingredients in a large bowl. Toss with dressing. Place sweet potatoes on top right before serving.

When I made a Kiddush for a new baby, I was sent many cakes, cookies, and petit fours. Amid all the sweets, this salad arrived. It was much enjoyed by my whole extended family who came to celebrate with us.

OLIVE-TOMATO SALAD

PAREVE . YIELDS 8 SERVINGS

½ (15-ounce) can black pitted olives, drained

½ (15-ounce) can green pitted olives, drained

1 pint grape tomatoes

DRESSING

1 Tablespoon olive oil

1 teaspoon salt

½ teaspoon pepper

1 clove garlic, crushed

1 cube frozen basil OR 1 teaspoon dried basil

1 **Prepare the dressing:** In a large bowl or container, combine dressing ingredients.

2 Add olives and tomatoes; toss gently. Allow to rest for 10 minutes to combine flavors.

A cousin of mine gave me a great tip for this recipe. When blended to a smooth consistency, it makes a delicious, perfectly spiced tomato dip.

TOMATO BASIL SALAD

PAREVE . YIELDS 5 SERVINGS

1 pint grape tomatoes, halved

DRESSING

⅓ cup oil

2 teaspoons salt

1 teaspoon dried basil OR one cube frozen basil

1 Tablespoon minced garlic

½ teaspoon black pepper

sprinkle of parsley

1 Place halved grape tomatoes into a bowl.

2 **Prepare the dressing:** Place dressing ingredients into a small jar. Shake well to combine.

3 Pour over tomatoes. Toss gently.

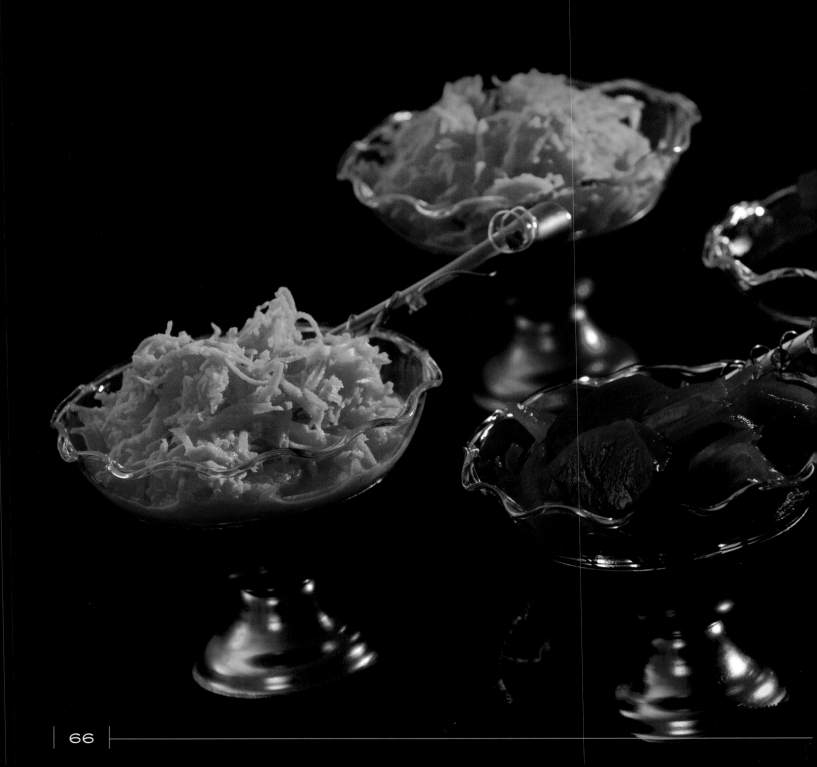

On a recent visit to Israel, I enjoyed the "salatim" that I was served with the first course. These salads keep well in the refrigerator, so you can pull them out for any meal that needs a filler. The vibrant colors provide visual appeal as well.

CARROT SALAD

PAREVE . YIELDS 10 SERVINGS

1 pound carrots,
peeled and grated

1 bunch scallions, sliced

DRESSING

3 Tablespoons lemon juice

3 Tablespoons sugar

3 Tablespoons mayonnaise

¼ teaspoon salt

1 Add carrots and scallions to a large bowl or container.

2 Prepare the dressing: Combine dressing ingredients in a small container.

3 Pour dressing over carrots and scallions. Toss to combine thoroughly.

4 Store covered tightly in the refrigerator.

BEET SALAD

PAREVE . YIELDS 10 SERVINGS

5 beets, tops stripped

2 medium red onions, cut vertically into thin strips

DRESSING

2 Tablespoons sugar

⅓ cup vinegar

2 teaspoons salt

⅔ cup water

1 Bring a 3-quart pot of salted water to a boil. Add unpeeled beets and boil until soft, 30-40 minutes. When cool enough to handle, slip off peels. (Use disposable gloves to avoid staining your hands.) Slice beets.

2 In a small saucepan, place onions in water to cover. Cook for 5 minutes; drain.

3 Prepare the dressing: Combine dressing ingredients in a small container.

4 Toss dressing with vegetables to coat. Refrigerate several hours before serving.

I served this at a Shabbos meal to my sister-in-law and her family. She took one look and made a face of displeasure at the ingredients. Then she tasted it. Then she cleaned her plate. Then she collected what was left on her children's plates. When she went into the kitchen to look for extras, I knew we had a winner!

SPINACH SALAD

PAREVE . YIELDS 8 SERVINGS

8 ounces baby spinach leaves	**DRESSING**
6 mushrooms, cleaned and sliced	4 Tablespoons oil
2 hard-boiled eggs, cut into ¼-inch slices	1 Tablespoon mayonnaise
2 scallions, diced	1 Tablespoon vinegar
	½ teaspoon salt
	3 shakes pepper

1 **Prepare the dressing:** Combine dressing ingredients in a small container and shake well.

2 Arrange salad ingredients on plates (see photo).

3 Drizzle dressing over salad.

The key to a successful potato salad is to dress it while it's warm.

VANISHING POTATO SALAD

PAREVE . YIELDS 8 SERVINGS

4 potatoes

3 sour pickles

4 scallions

2 carrots, grated

DRESSING

6 Tablespoons mayonnaise

2 teaspoons vinegar

1 teaspoon salt

black pepper, to taste

1 Cook potatoes in skins, in salted water, until easily pierced with a fork (about 25 minutes). Pour off water and wait until cool enough to handle. Peel and cut into cubes.

2 Dice sour pickles finely. Slice scallions into ¼-inch slices. Combine with potatoes and grated carrots.

3 **Prepare the dressing:** In a separate bowl, combine dressing ingredients. Using an immersion blender will yield a creamier dressing.

4 Pour over salad and mix well.

Peeling the kirbies will not alter the taste, but the presentations is a bit nicer and the texture a bit crispier with the peels.

RUSSIAN COLE SLAW

PAREVE . YIELDS 10-12 SERVINGS

10	kirbies, unpeeled	**DRESSING**
1	teaspoon salt	¼ cup vinegar
8	small red radishes, plus 2 for garnish	⅓ cup sugar
		4 Tablespoons mayonnaise
4	scallions	1 teaspoon salt
½	bunch fresh dill	

1 Using a food processor, shred kirbies coarsely. Place in a bowl and salt lightly. Let stand for 15 minutes so excess liquid is expressed. Press out and discard excess liquid.

2 Using the same blade used for kirbies, shred 8 radishes. Slice scallions thinly and snip dill finely with kitchen shears. Combine with drained kirbies and radishes.

3 **Prepare the dressing:** Using a food processor or immersion blender, combine all dressing ingredients.

4 Pour over salad and toss gently to coat. Slice remaining 2 radishes thinly into rounds to garnish.

PARSLEY MANDARIN SALAD

PAREVE . YIELDS 10-12 SERVINGS

I consider myself somewhat of a salad connoisseur. As such, I couldn't believe that there was a lettuce salad out there that I had never seen or tasted. Then I found this one! The medley of tastes and textures creates a winning combination. Try it once; you will definitely get requests for an encore.

2 (8-ounce) bags lettuce

1½ (11-ounce) cans mandarin oranges, drained

½ red onion, diced

2 stalks celery, diced

½ cup sugared slivered almonds

DRESSING

¼ cup oil

2 Tablespoons sugar

2 Tablespoons red wine vinegar

2 Tablespoons dried parsley

½ teaspoon salt

¼ teaspoon pepper

1 In a large bowl, combine all salad ingredients.

2 **Prepare the dressing:** Add dressing ingredients to a small jar or covered container. Shake well or use an immersion blender to combine.

3 Pour dressing over salad and toss.

Make your own sugared almonds:

½ cup slivered almonds

1½ Tablespoons white sugar

1 Stir sugar over medium heat until melted. Continue stirring over heat until brown (watch carefully, because it burns easily).

2 Turn off heat and stir in nuts.

3 Spread in a thin layer on a baking sheet lined with parchment paper.

4 Break apart when cool.

We make this weekly for Shabbos; my kids never seem to tire of it.

TOMATO-ASPARAGUS SALAD

PAREVE . YIELDS 8-10 SERVINGS

1 (16-ounce) bag frozen cut asparagus

½ pint grape tomatoes, whole or halved

1 (15-ounce) can hearts of palm, drained

1 small red onion

DRESSING

⅓ cup oil

¼ cup vinegar

1 teaspoon salt

¼ cup sugar

2 cloves garlic, crushed

1 teaspoon imitation mustard

1 Defrost asparagus in advance. Drain any excess water. Pat dry with paper towels.

2 Cut grape tomatoes in half if desired.

3 Slice hearts of palm and red onion into rounds.

4 **Prepare the dressing:** Combine all ingredients in a small jar. Shake well or use an immersion blender to combine.

5 Pour dressing over salad immediately before serving.

My kids love all things "hot"; they eat hot peppers straight from the jar. These salads are a step up in sophistication for the "hot" lovers, young and old. Use disposable gloves when dicing jalapeño peppers. The matbucha freezes well. Pour into 1-pound containers and freeze.

MOROCCAN MATBUCHA

PAREVE

10 very large, very ripe beef tomatoes, diced	1 head garlic, crushed
1 (28-ounce) can crushed tomatoes	2 teaspoons salt
	1 teaspoon paprika
2 green peppers, diced	2 Tablespoons oil
	4 jalapeño peppers, diced

Place all ingredients into a large pot. Cover and cook over low heat until soft, about 1 hour. Uncover and cook 2-3 hours, stirring occasionally, until liquid cooks off.

MUHAMARRA

PAREVE

1 (12-ounce) jar red peppers	2 Tablespoons olive oil
2 cloves garlic	2 teaspoons lemon juice
1 cup chopped walnuts	¼ teaspoon cayenne pepper
½ cup potato starch OR matzo meal*	½ teaspoon salt

Place ingredients in the bowl of a food processor fitted with the S-blade. Process until combined, but leave it chunky enough to retain texture.

*Using matzo meal will make this *gebrokts*.

HOT PEPPER SALAD

PAREVE

1 Tablespoon oil	½ yellow pepper, sliced
1 onion, diced	
	½ teaspoon salt
½ red pepper, sliced	
	1 (16-oz) jar hot peppers, drained
½ orange pepper, sliced	

Heat oil in a skillet over medium-high heat. Add onion and sauté until translucent. Add peppers and salt; sauté until tender, about 10 minutes. Add hot peppers and cook additional 5 minutes.

FISH

HERBED SALMON
WITH MANGO-PINEAPPLE SALSA

PAREVE . YIELDS 8 SERVINGS

8　(1½-inch slices) salmon fillets

½　cup lemon juice

4　cups water

½　Tablespoon salt

½　cup mayonnaise

SEASONING BLEND

1　teaspoon oregano

1　teaspoon dried basil

1　teaspoon dill weed

2　teaspoons kosher salt

1½　teaspoons garlic powder

¼　teaspoon black pepper

½　teaspoon dried parsley

1　teaspoon minced dried onion flakes

MANGO-PINEAPPLE SALSA

1　cup mango, diced small

1　cup pineapple, diced small

1　small red onion, diced small

½　cup red pepper, diced small

2　Tablespoons vinegar

1　Tablespoon olive oil

　salt and pepper, to taste

1　**Prepare the seasoning blend:** Combine the herbs and spices in a small bowl.

2　**Prepare the fish:** Combine the lemon juice, water, and salt in a large shallow bowl. Marinate the salmon in the lemon bath for half an hour.

3　Preheat oven to 425°F. Remove salmon from lemon bath. Place the salmon, skin side down, onto a baking sheet. Spread the mayonnaise over the salmon, covering it completely.

4　Sprinkle seasoning blend generously over the salmon. Bake, covered, for 15 minutes. Uncover; bake an additional 10 minutes.

5　Toss salsa ingredients together. Serve over warm or room-temperature salmon.

Very delicious and easy to prepare.
While we think the salsa is a fabulous pair to
the salmon, this fish is definitely tasty enough
to serve solo.

This photo shows the seared tuna logs, ready to be cut into slices for the presentation above.

SEARED TUNA
WITH AVOCADO AND SPICY MAYO

PAREVE . YIELDS 12 SERVINGS

¾ pound fresh tuna, cut into logs (see picture)

2 Tablespoons salt

pepper, to taste

2 Tablespoons olive oil

AVOCADO MASH

2 ripe avocados

salt, to taste

pepper, to taste

1 Tablespoon olive oil

SPICY MAYO

1 cup mayonnaise

3¼ ounces water

½ cup ketchup

1 Tablespoon sugar

1½ teaspoons hot pepper flakes

1 cube frozen garlic OR 1 clove garlic, crushed

⅓ teaspoon paprika

⅛ teaspoon white pepper

⅛ teaspoon salt

1 **Prepare spicy mayo:** Combine ingredients in container and blend with an immersion blender.

2 **Prepare the fish:** Rub tuna with salt and pepper. Grease medium skillet lightly and heat over medium-high flame until hot. Sear tuna on each side. Leave the center as pink as desired: For rare 3-4 minutes per side, for medium 5-6 minutes per side, and for well-done 8-9 minutes per side. Remove from heat; cool. Slice into ¼-inch slices.

3 **Prepare the avocado mash:** Scoop out avocado flesh and mash it with salt, pepper, and olive oil. Set aside in an airtight container.

4 Serve tuna with avocado and spicy mayo.

To plate as shown, place 3 cucumber rounds on each plate. Place one tablespoon avocado mash on each round; top each with a slice of tuna and a dollop of spicy mayo.

Since we created this recipe, it has shown up at each of our Shabbos tables consistently. Different, delicious, and beautiful enough to "wow" your guests.

SPINACH-SALMON SPIRALS

PAREVE . YIELDS 20 SERVINGS

1 side of salmon, butterflied

1 loaf gefilte fish, defrosted

2 Tablespoons oil

2 onions, diced

1 cup frozen spinach, thawed

salt

pepper

garlic powder

onion powder

1 Heat oil in a skillet over medium heat. Add onions and sauté until soft. Add frozen spinach and spices, to taste, Cook for 2-3 minutes. Remove from heat.

2 Drain the excess liquid. In a large bowl, combine spinach mixture with defrosted gefilte fish.

3 Spread gefilte fish mixture over salmon. Roll salmon jelly roll style. Freeze overnight.

4 Remove salmon roll from freezer and let thaw slightly. Preheat oven to 350°F. Grease a baking sheet. Cut salmon roll into ½-inch slices and place on prepared baking sheet. Bake for 25 minutes.

A super recipe — gorgeous, easy and yields a large quantity.
Note: Any extra filling can be baked in individual muffin tins.

Serve with dill dip: 1 cup mayonnaise, 4 cubes frozen dill, 1 Tablespoon lemon juice, 1 clove garlic (crushed), salt and pepper to taste. Blend.

An elegant start to your
Yom Tov meal.

The garnish is easy to replicate
and will finish your plate
nicely. With a mandolin or
regular vegetable peeler,
peel an English (seedless)
cucumber along the side into
long strips. Wrap one entire
strip around three fingers,
then slip off carefully to retain
the shape. Stuff with assorted
greens or pepper strips.

MUSHROOM-STUFFED SOLE

PAREVE . YIELDS 6 SERVINGS

6   (4-ounce) fillets of sole

2   large ripe tomatoes, chopped OR 1 (15-ounce) can diced tomatoes

2   cloves garlic, minced

½   cup white wine

1   teaspoon lemon juice

    salt, to taste

    pepper, to taste

    basil, optional

MUSHROOM STUFFING

1   pound fresh mushrooms, coarsely chopped

2   Tablespoons chopped scallions

1   small clove garlic, minced

2   Tablespoons oil

    salt, to taste

    pepper, to taste

    parsley, optional

1   Preheat oven to 350°F. Prepare a 9 x 13" baking pan.

2   Combine ingredients for mushroom stuffing. Place 2-3 tablespoons stuffing on each fillet and roll fish around stuffing. Secure with a toothpick if necessary. Place fish rolls in pan, seam side down.

3   Mix tomatoes with garlic and spread over fish. Pour wine and lemon juice over fish. Sprinkle with salt, pepper, and basil. Spray with nonstick cooking spray.

4   Bake, covered, for 30 minutes. Uncover and bake for additional 10 minutes.

You can't get more traditional than homemade gefilte fish! My childhood Pesach memories include a warm piece of homemade gefilte fish straight out of the pot.

For homemade Pesach mayo: Blend 1½ tablespoons sugar, 2 raw eggs, 1 hard-boiled egg, 4 Tablespoons lemon juice, a sliver of onion, salt, and pepper. With blender running, add 1 cup oil v-e-r-y s-l-o-w-l-y in a thin stream. To thicken, add more oil.

TRADITIONAL GEFILTE FISH

PAREVE . YIELDS 25-30 SERVINGS

FISH

1½ pounds ground whitefish

1½ pounds ground pike

1 large onion, ground

1 carrot, ground

6 eggs

¾ cup sugar

⅛ cup kosher salt

1 teaspoon garlic powder

1½ Tablespoons potato starch

STOCK

water as needed

2 Tablespoons salt

1 cup sugar

2 large carrots, peeled

1 onion, sliced

1 **Prepare the fish mixture:** Place all fish ingredients into a mixing bowl. Combine well using an electric mixer at medium speed for 10-15 minutes. Refrigerate mixture overnight, covered.

2 **Prepare the stock:** Add water to a 10-quart pot to come ⅔ up the sides. Add salt and sugar. Add whole carrots and sliced onion. Bring to a boil.

3 Remove fish from refrigerator. Wet hands and form fist-size ovals of fish. Drop fish ovals into boiling water.

4 Return to boil, then lower to a simmer. With cover slightly ajar, cook for 45 minutes to 1 hour. Chill before serving.

Variation 1: To form loaves instead of individual balls, bring water, salt and sugar to a boil in a large roasting pan (you may have to set it over two flames). Add onion and carrots. Wet hands; form 2 fish loaves and place into boiling water. When water returns to a boil, lower heat and simmer for 90 minutes.

Variation 2: To make fried fish balls, as pictured, heat ¼-inch oil in a frying pan. Scoop raw fish mixture with a melon baller or teaspoon and drop into hot oil. Fry 2 minutes on each side and remove with a slotted spoon.

SALMON IN CREAM SAUCE

PAREVE . YIELDS 8 SERVINGS

8 (3-4-ounce) slices salmon fillet, skin removed	**DRESSING**
	½ cup water
1 medium onion, sliced into rings	½ cup mayonnaise
	½ cup ketchup
2 bay leaves	½ cup vinegar
	½ cup sugar

If your fillet has the skin on, it can be difficult to remove when it is raw. Cook salmon skin side up in water (Step 1) and pour off water. Remove skin while fish is warm. It should come off easily. Turn fillets over and continue with Step 2.

1 Place fish into an 8-quart pot. Add water to cover and place over a medium-high flame. Bring to a boil, then reduce to a simmer. Cook for 25 minutes. Carefully pour off water. Fish may be transferred to a storage dish at this point.

2 Place onion rings over fish. Blend dressing ingredients and pour over salmon, making sure surfaces of the fish are completely covered.

3 Place bay leaves into the sauce at opposite ends of dish.

4 Cover and refrigerate. Serve chilled.

MOROCCAN WHITEFISH

PAREVE . YIELDS 8 SERVINGS

My Moroccan neighbor who shared this recipe makes it regularly with salmon as well.

8   (1-inch) whitefish steaks

1   (28-ounce) can crushed tomatoes

8   cloves garlic, crushed

2   large carrots, cut into spears

4   jalapeño peppers, seeded and each cut into 4 spears

1   Tablespoon salt (or to taste)

½   cup oil

2   teaspoons paprika

1   teaspoon hot paprika

    dried parsley

1   lemon

1   Place ingredients into an 8-quart pot, layering as follows: crushed tomatoes, garlic, carrots, jalapeño pepper. Sprinkle generously with salt. (To tone down the spiciness, use only 2 jalapeño peppers and substitute regular paprika for the hot paprika in Step 3.)

2   Place fish slices over layers.

3   In a small bowl, mix oil with both types of paprika and drizzle over fish.

4   Sprinkle with parsley. Slice lemon into four thin slices. Cut each slice in half, and place over parsley on each fish steak.

5   Cover pot, place over medium-low flame, and slowly bring to a boil (about 10 minutes). Cook for an additional 30-45 minutes, shaking pot 2-3 times during cooking to combine flavors. Serve warm or at room temperature.

This method of broiling salmon makes for the perfect texture every time. It can be used for any of your favorite salmon recipes.

MR. UNGAR'S SALMON

P A R E V E . Y I E L D S 6 S E R V I N G S

6   (1½-inch) slices very fresh salmon fillet (not frozen)

    olive oil

½   cup lime OR lemon juice

½   cup sweet OR semisweet white wine

    kosher salt, for sprinkling

    garlic powder, for sprinkling

1   Pour a thin layer of olive oil into a 9 x 13" pan, preferably a heavyweight aluminum one. Place salmon into pan, skin side up.

2   Pour lime (or lemon) juice and wine over fish; the liquid should come up about ¼-inch in the pan.

3   Broil the fish directly under the heating element on high for 4-5 minutes, leaving the oven door slightly ajar. This will ensure the salmon broils nicely, as opposed to baking.

4   Remove from broiler. Skin the salmon and flip the fillets right side up. Sprinkle fillets with kosher salt and garlic powder.

5   Return to broiler for additional 4-5 minutes. The salmon will be slightly darker pink in the center. Remove from broiler and immediately cover tightly with foil. This will allow the fish to continue cooking until it is completely cooked to perfection.

Note: The salmon SHOULD look slightly raw when taking out of the broiler! The trick is to have faith; if it is kept covered it WILL continue cooking.

When you've had your share of salmon, sea bass is a welcome change. It has such a rich flavor that I use it as an entrée for a meatless meal, and my guests are just as satisfied.

CHILEAN SEA BASS

PAREVE . YIELDS 4 SERVINGS

4	(1-inch appetizer or 1½-inch main dish portions) sea bass fillets	salt, to taste
		pepper, to taste
2	Tablespoons oil	**OIL/SPICE MIXTURE**
2	large onions, diced	3 Tablespoons olive oil
1	(10-ounce) box mushrooms, cleaned and sliced	salt, to taste
		pepper, to taste
5	cloves garlic, crushed	garlic powder
1	cup fresh cilantro OR 7 cubes frozen cilantro	barbecue seasoning, to taste (we like Pereg brand)

1 Preheat oven to 350°F.

2 While oven is heating, heat oil in a large skillet over a medium-high flame. Sauté onions until translucent. Add mushrooms and sauté till soft. Add garlic, cilantro, salt, and pepper. Remove from heat.

3 In a small bowl, mix olive oil, salt, pepper, garlic powder, and barbecue seasoning. Smear fish with oil/spice mixture. Place into a 9 x 13" baking dish.

4 Pour onion mixture over fish. Bake, uncovered, for 20-30 minutes. Serve warm or at room temperature.

SOLE WITH SUN-DRIED TOMATOES

PAREVE . YIELDS 6 SERVINGS

6	sole fillets
12	sun-dried tomatoes packed in oil, chopped
6	Tablespoons olive oil
5	cloves garlic, minced
	salt, to taste
	pepper, to taste

1 Place all ingredients into a large ziplock bag. Marinate in the refrigerator for 3-4 hours or overnight.

2 Preheat oven to 350°F. Transfer fish to a baking dish, discarding marinade. Bake, covered, 15-20 minutes.

To make your own sun-dried tomatoes, preheat oven to 175°F. Slice tomatoes in half and place, cut side up, on a lined baking sheet. Combine equal amounts salt and sugar and sprinkle over tomatoes. Bake, uncovered, for 10 hours.

TILAPIA WITH VEGETABLES

PAREVE . YIELDS 6 SERVINGS

2 Tablespoons oil

1 medium onion, diced

1 red pepper, diced

1 yellow pepper, diced

1 small zucchini,
  peeled and diced

1 beef tomato, diced

10 ounces mushrooms,
   cleaned and sliced

1 clove garlic, crushed

1 teaspoon paprika

¼ teaspoon black pepper

salt, to taste

6 tilapia fillets

2 Tablespoons lemon juice

salt

pepper

1 **Prepare the vegetables:** In a large skillet, heat oil over medium heat. Add onion and sauté until translucent, 7-10 minutes. Add peppers and zucchini and sauté for additional 20 minutes, stirring often. Add tomato; continue to sauté for 5 minutes. Add mushrooms, garlic, paprika, pepper, and salt; sauté for another 3 minutes, until all vegetables are fork-tender. Set aside.

2 **Prepare the fish:** Place tilapia fillets, in a single layer, into a large roasting pan. Sprinkle with lemon juice, salt, and pepper. Cover and bake at 350°F for 5 minutes.

3 Spread vegetable mixture over fish. Bake, covered, at 350°F for 30 minutes.

This recipe can also be made with sea bass; just add ten minutes to the cooking time.

To make in advance, prepare the fish and vegetables in a pan and freeze before the second baking.

My father's pet peeve is overcooked salmon. This
unconventional method of preparing the salmon
will get it perfect every time.
Pronounced "seh-VEE-chay," it is a popular cooking
method in the Central and South America.

SALMON CEVICHE

PAREVE . YIELDS 4 SERVINGS

3   (6-ounce) salmon fillets, skin removed

½   cup vinegar

½   cup sugar (or more to taste)

1   cup lemon juice

1   cup water

2   bay leaves

1   Cut fish fillets into 1-inch cubes. Place fish cubes in a single layer in a 9 x 13" pan. Prepare a piece of heavy-duty foil to cover the pan, with some overhang.

2   In a saucepan over high heat, bring remaining ingredients to a rapid boil. Working quickly, pour hot liquid over fish cubes. Immediately cover pan loosely with prepared foil. (Don't crimp around edges of pan yet.)

3   Place a second (empty) 9 x 13" pan over foil-covered fish and place something heavy into pan to weigh it down. Now crimp edges of foil around fish pan to seal tightly.

4   Refrigerate fish in the pans, with the weight, and marinate for 24-48 hours.

The salmon is ready to eat; no further cooking is necessary.

PICKLED WHITEFISH

*An old classic — redone.
Simple to prepare and delicious!*

PAREVE . YIELDS 6 SERVINGS

6	(1-inch-thick) whitefish steaks
2	medium onions, sliced
2	teaspoons salt
1	teaspoon allspice
½	cup sugar
½	cup vinegar
1½	cups water
2	bay leaves

1 In a 3-quart pot, combine onions, salt, allspice, sugar, vinegar, water, and bay leaves.

2 Place fish slices into mixture. Refrigerate overnight.

3 Remove from refrigerator. Cook for 1½ hours over medium flame.

4 Chill. Serve with jellied fish sauce.

Every time I make supper, I find that half my family loves it and half is scrounging in the fridge for an alternative. At my friend's suggestion, I started making two completely different sauces for the main dish: one sweet and one tart. It worked! Now everyone is happy, including me.

CHICKEN NUGGETS WITH TWO SAUCES

MEAT . YIELDS 12 SERVINGS

3 pounds chicken cutlets, cut into bite-size nuggets	1 Combine batter ingredients in a large bowl.
oil for frying	2 Heat a layer of oil in heavy skillet.
BATTER	3 Dip cutlets in batter to coat. When oil is hot, fry on both sides until golden. Serve plain or with your choice of sauces, below.
4 eggs	
4 Tablespoons water	
1½ cups potato starch	
1 teaspoon salt	

SWEET & PUNGENT SAUCE

1 Tablespoon oil

1 large onion, diced

1 large green pepper, diced

1 (8-ounce) can mushrooms

¾ cup brown sugar

¾ cup ketchup

¾ cup water

1 Heat oil in a small saucepan. Add onion and green pepper and sauté until soft. Add remaining ingredients; bring to a boil. Serve as dipping sauce with chicken nuggets.

Variation: Pour sauce over fried cutlets and bake in a preheated oven, uncovered, at 350°F for ½ hour.

LEMON SAUCE

4 Tablespoons oil

8 Tablespoons lemon juice

8 Tablespoons sugar

6 Tablespoons vinegar

1½ cups chicken broth

4 teaspoons potato starch

½ teaspoon salt

1 Heat oil in saucepan.

2 While oil is heating, combine remaining ingredients in bowl. Add to oil. Bring to a boil and cook until thickened. Serve as a dipping sauce with chicken nuggets.

Variation: Pour sauce over fried cutlets and bake in a preheated oven, uncovered, at 350°F for ½ hour.

PASTRAMI AND SPINACH STUFFED CHICKEN

MEAT . YIELDS 8 SERVINGS

1 Tablespoon oil

32 ounces frozen chopped spinach, thawed

1 large onion, finely diced

3 cloves garlic, minced

salt, to taste

pepper, to taste

8 dark chicken cutlets (deboned chicken thighs)

½ pound pastrami, cut into strips

DRESSING
½ cup ketchup

½ cup duck sauce

1 Preheat oven to 350°F.

2 Heat oil in a skillet. Sauté onion in oil over medium-high heat until translucent. Add spinach and garlic; cook for 5 minutes. Add salt and pepper. Stir until smooth. Remove from heat and drain off as much liquid as possible.

3 Place a chicken cutlet on work surface, underside up. Spread a 1-inch-wide strip of spinach mixture down the center. Place strips of pastrami over spinach mixture. Fold both sides of cutlet over center. Place seam side down in a 9 x 13" pan. Repeat with remaining cutlets.

4 Combine dressing ingredients in a bowl and pour over prepared stuffed cutlets in pan. Cover and bake for 1 hour and 45 minutes.

I ate this at a Shabbos Sheva Berachos and went straight to the kitchen to get the recipe. The caterer was flattered and shared it with me. When I make this for my family I make some without spinach for the people who will not eat anything green (like my husband!).

DUCK À L'ORANGE

MEAT . YIELDS 4 SERVINGS

To create the pictured garnish, reserve ¼ cup of glaze. Slice an orange and place it on a parchment paper-lined baking sheet. Brush with glaze and bake at 550°F for 3 minutes.

This recipe tastes just as good using Cornish hens or chicken quarters.

1 duck
  (about 4.5 pounds)

¼ teaspoon onion powder

¼ teaspoon garlic powder

  salt, to taste

  pepper, to taste

½ teaspoon paprika

GLAZE

1 cup orange juice

½ cup honey

2 Tablespoons lemon juice

½ cup duck sauce

1 clove fresh garlic

¼ cup sherry

1 Tablespoon apricot jam

1 Preheat oven to 350°F.

2 Place duck in a large pot and add water to cover. Bring to a boil. Remove after 5-10 minutes. Clean skin, trim away fat, and remove pin feathers.

3 Place duck in a large roasting pan. Rub with onion powder, garlic powder, salt, pepper, and paprika.

4 Cover tightly and bake for 1½ hours.

5 Meanwhile, combine glaze ingredients in a small saucepan. Bring to a boil, stirring frequently until smooth.

6 When duck is roasted, remove from oven and drain drippings. Pour sauce over duck. Cover pan. Bake ½ hour, covered. Bake additional ½ hour, uncovered.

My favorites were crunchy cabbage salad, Pecan crusted chicken, potato meat kugel and pear thank you again

The pecan-coated shnitzel was very good.

When I heard "Pecan Chicken," I envisioned chicken quarters with whole pecans in a brown-sugar sauce. So, when I opened the package labeled "Pecan Chicken" at the photo shoot, I was taken by surprise! One bite confirmed that this chicken was perfectly moist on the inside and crispy on the outside, with an all-around palate-pleasing taste. Different from what I expected, but oh, so much better!

PECAN-CRUSTED CHICKEN

MEAT . YIELDS 4 SERVINGS

4   chicken cutlets, pounded thin

1   egg white, lightly beaten

    oil, for frying

COATING

¾   cup chopped pecans

4   Tablespoons potato starch

½   teaspoon salt

    dash pepper

    oil, for frying

1   Place beaten egg white into a shallow bowl. Combine coating
    ingredients in a second shallow bowl.

2   Dip cutlets into beaten egg white, then into pecan mixture
    to coat.

3   Heat oil in a skillet over medium flame. Fry about 6 minutes on
    each side.

VEAL-STUFFED CORNISH HEN
WITH CHERRY SAUCE

A great variation for this recipe is to use chicken capons (deboned chicken bottoms) instead of cornish hens.

MEAT . YIELDS 8 SERVINGS

8 (1-pound) Cornish hens

garlic powder

VEAL MIXTURE

2 Tablespoons oil

1 onion, diced

10 ounces fresh mushrooms, sliced

¾ pound ground veal

2 eggs

2 Tablespoons potato starch

CHERRY SAUCE

1 (15-ounce) can sweet pitted cherries

2 Tablespoons sugar

¼ teaspoon salt

1 Tablespoon potato starch dissolved in 4 Tablespoons water

1 **Prepare veal stuffing:** Heat oil in a skillet. Sauté onions and mushrooms in oil over medium-high heat until soft. Remove from heat. Add ground veal, eggs, and potato starch. Mix thoroughly to combine.

2 Preheat oven to 400°F.

3 Stuff Cornish hens with veal mixture. Place into a roasting pan and sprinkle with garlic powder.

4 Cover and bake at 400°F for 30 minutes; then lower temperature to 350°F and bake for an additional 20 minutes. Uncover pan and bake for 15 minutes more.

5 **Meanwhile, prepare cherry sauce:** Drain the liquid from the can of cherries into a saucepan. Set aside cherries. Set saucepan over medium-high heat. Add sugar, salt, and potato starch mixture. Bring to a boil. Cook, stirring occasionally, until thickened. Remove from heat and stir in reserved cherries.

6 Pour cherry sauce over hens immediately before serving.

My mother's friend Beth is a great cook. This is her no-fail recipe for Chicken Marsala. What's great is that it can be prepared in advance and frozen.

CHICKEN MARSALA

MEAT . YIELDS 6 SERVINGS

6 dark chicken cutlets (substitute white if preferred)

potato starch

olive oil

10 ounces fresh mushrooms, sliced

3 cloves garlic, minced or crushed

¼ cup white wine

2 teaspoons lemon juice

1 cup chicken stock

salt, to taste

pepper, to taste

1 Preheat oven to 350°F.

2 Dredge cutlets in potato starch.

3 Heat olive oil in a large skillet over medium-high heat. Fry cutlets in olive oil until chicken is no longer pink.

4 Place fried chicken into a 9 x 13" pan. Using the same skillet, sauté mushrooms and garlic until browned. Add wine, lemon juice, stock, salt, and pepper to vegetables. Bring to a boil.

5 Pour sauce over chicken. (Chicken can be frozen at this point. Add 25 minutes to baking time if baking frozen chicken.)

6 Bake, covered, for 30 minutes.

If you love fried onions,
but don't love actually standing
and frying them, you'll appreciate
this recipe. The fried-onion taste
is so authentic, you might
fool yourself!

The onion soup mix can be
substituted with a mixture of salt,
pepper, garlic powder, onion
powder, and paprika, to taste.

ONION CHICKEN

MEAT . YIELDS 6 SERVINGS

6   chicken legs

¼   cup olive oil + 2 Tablespoons

3   Tablespoons onion soup mix

3   large onions, thinly sliced

    salt, to taste

    pepper, to taste

    paprika, to taste

1   Preheat oven to 375°F. Lightly grease 9 x 13" pan.

2   Into a large ziplock bag, place ¼ cup oil, onion soup mix, and sliced onions. Shake to combine.

3   Place ¼ of mixture from bag into prepared pan. Add chicken. Season chicken with salt, pepper, and paprika. Pour remaining mixture over chicken. Drizzle with 2 tablespoons olive oil. Cover pan.

4   Bake 1 hour. Uncover pan; bake additional ½ hour, until topmost onions are crispy.

When I lived in Israel, turkey was the only "meat" available. Since I had an open-house policy, with bachurim frequently eating over, I have tried many turkey recipes — but I must say that this is my favorite. Easy, tasty, and always finished to the last morsel!

TURKEY ROULADE

MEAT . YIELDS ABOUT 8 SERVINGS

1 Tablespoon oil

1 large onion, diced

2 cloves garlic, sliced

1 (3-pound) turkey roulade

½ cup semi-sweet red wine

½ cup ketchup

3 Tablespoons onion soup mix (or use spice mix in the note on page 108)

¼ teaspoon onion powder

½ teaspoon paprika

1½ cups water

1 Heat oil in a deep saucepan. Sauté onion and garlic in oil until translucent. Add turkey and sauté for 2 minutes.

2 Add red wine, pouring around perimeter of pot, not directly over turkey. Simmer for 2-3 minutes. Turn roulade over; add remaining ingredients.

3 Bring to a boil, then immediately reduce to a simmer. Cover pot and cook 2 hours, turning roulade occasionally.

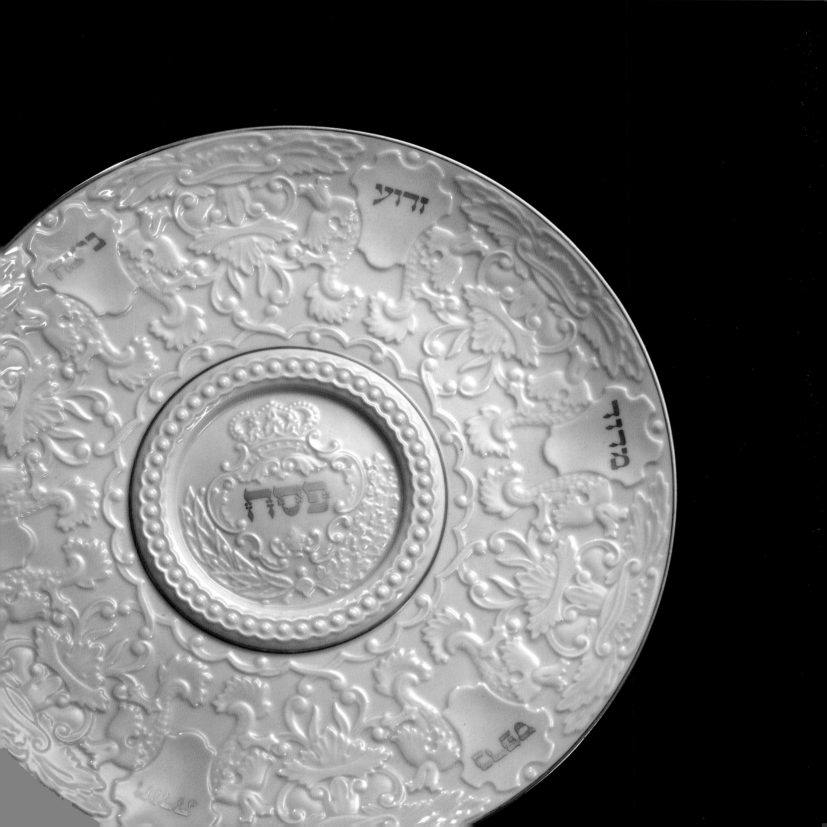

ONION-TOPPED FRENCH ROAST

MEAT . YIELDS 8-10 SERVINGS

1   (4-pound) French roast

3   large onions

    oil for frying

SPICE RUB

2   Tablespoons onion soup mix (to make your own, see page 108)

2   teaspoons paprika

½   teaspoon black pepper

4   Tablespoons olive oil

4   cloves garlic, chopped

1   Combine ingredients for spice rub and smear liberally on all sides of roast. Wrap in foil and refrigerate overnight, or at least 5 hours.

2   Preheat oven to 500°F. Place wrapped roast into a large pan. Cover pan tightly. Bake for half an hour.

3   Reduce heat to 325°F and bake an additional 2 hours. Allow to cool completely, then slice.

4   Slice onions into rings and sauté in 2 tablespoons oil until golden brown. Arrange over sliced roast in pan.

5   Before serving, bake covered at 350°F for 45 minutes.

I picked up a French roast from the butcher to prepare for Shabbos. Since I didn't want to make an additional stop at the grocery, I challenged myself to come up with a moist, flavorful recipe using only ingredients I had in my house. I knew I passed the test when I had no leftovers to package after the meal.

One of the committee members has been suggesting unstuffed cabbage for the cookbook for the last 3 years. The rest of us were hesitant to include a recipe that would not make a nice presentation. We were pleasantly surprised that besides tasting delicious, it served beautifully.

UNSTUFFED CABBAGE

MEAT . YIELDS 12 SERVINGS

2 (8-ounce) packages shredded green cabbage

1 (16-ounce) jar sauerkraut, drained

MEAT MIXTURE

2 pounds ground meat

2 eggs

4 Tablespoons ketchup

   salt, to taste

   pepper, to taste

   onion powder, to taste

SAUCE

1 large Spanish onion, diced

2 (15-ounce) cans tomato sauce

2¾ cups water

½ cup brown sugar

1 Preheat oven to 350°F.

2 Combine meat mixture ingredients. Set aside.

3 In a saucepan, sauté onion until translucent. Add remaining sauce ingredients and bring to a boil over medium heat. Simmer for a few minutes.

4 In a 9 x 13" pan, layer ingredients in this order:
   1 bag of cabbage
   meat mixture
   sauerkraut
   remaining bag of cabbage.

5 Pour sauce over layers.

6 Bake, covered, 2½ hours.

TANGY ENGLISH RIBS

The term "English ribs" means that the ribs are separated from one another along the bone and the meat is on top. My butcher has them ready packaged in his showcase, but any butcher can prepare ribs for you this way.

MEAT . YIELDS 4 SERVINGS

4   English ribs OR 8 short ribs

1   (15-ounce) can tomato sauce

2   cups water

5   Tablespoons brown sugar

3   bay leaves

1   Preheat oven to 300°F.

2   Place ribs into a 9 x 13" baking pan. Pour tomato sauce over the meat. Add 2 cups of water.

3   Sprinkle the brown sugar over the meat; add bay leaves.

4   Cover tightly and bake for 3-4 hours until the meat falls off the bone.

Bring out your favorite wine with this dish. We prefer a dry wine such as Merlot. The sweet sauce also works well with corned beef or your favorite pickled meat.

TONGUE WITH SWEET SAUCE

MEAT . YIELDS 8 SERVINGS

1	pickled tongue
1	medium onion, diced
2	Tablespoons oil
1	cup ketchup
⅔	cup brown sugar
⅓	cup raisins
¾	cup water

1 Place tongue into a large pot with water to cover; bring to a boil. After 5 minutes, pour off water. Cover tongue with water again, cover pot, and boil gently for 3 to 4 hours until tender. When tongue has cooled, peel it and slice thinly.

2 Heat oil in a large skillet over medium heat. Add onion and sauté for 5-10 minutes, until soft. Add remaining ingredients. Stir for 2-3 minutes until small bubbles form.

3 SERVING OPTIONS:

1. Add sliced tongue to sauce in skillet. Heat over medium heat until hot, about 10 minutes.

2. Prepare sauce (Step 2). Layer tongue slices in a 9 x 13″ pan and pour sauce over it. Heat in oven, covered, at 300°F for 20-30 minutes, until heated through.

Lamb meat is a great fit for a healthy diet, because lamb contains many essential nutrients. On average, a 3-ounce serving of lamb has only 175 calories, qualifying it as a lean meat. (And it's delicious too!)

LAMB CHOPS

MEAT . YIELDS 4 SERVINGS

4   (¾-inch thick) lamb chops

1   Tablespoon parsley flakes

4   frozen garlic cubes

    salt, to taste

    pepper, to taste

1   Tablespoon olive oil

¼   cup minced shallots

½   cup balsamic vinegar

¾   cup chicken broth

1   In a small bowl, combine parsley, garlic cubes, salt, and pepper. Rub the mixture onto the lamb chops on both sides. Place chops on a plate; cover and set aside for 15 minutes to absorb the flavors.

2   Heat olive oil in a large skillet over medium heat. Place lamb chops into the skillet and cook for about 3½ minutes per side for medium rare, or continue to cook until desired doneness. Remove from the skillet and keep warm on a serving platter.

3   Add shallots to the skillet and cook for a few minutes just until browned. Stir in vinegar, scraping any bits of lamb from the bottom of the skillet, and then stir in the chicken broth.

4   Continue to cook and stir over medium-high heat for about 5 minutes, until the sauce has been reduced by half, so that it is not too liquidy. Remove from heat and pour over lamb chops.

This has "upscale steakhouse" written all over it. It gives a whole new meaning to "meat and potatoes"! This can be prepared in stages for a Friday-evening meal. Sear steaks early in the day, then bake right before Shabbos. Turn off the oven and leave steaks in it until ready to serve.

STEAK STACK

MEAT . YIELDS 4 SERVINGS

Potato Kugel, page 141, OR
your favorite potato kugel recipe

4   rib steaks

     pepper, to taste

2   large onions, sliced into thin rounds

1   cup potato starch

     oil for frying and greasing

1   **Prepare potato kugel:** Preheat oven to 350°F. Divide batter into
     four well-greased 3" round tins, filling them slightly less than
     half-full, so that they will be flat after baking.

2   Bake mini kugels until golden, about 45 minutes.

3   While kugels are baking, lightly grease a grill pan and set over
     high heat. Season steaks with black pepper, place on heated
     grill pan, and sear for 4 minutes on each side. (Do this step
     in batches if necessary.) See note on facing page if preparing
     steaks in advance.

4   Transfer steaks to a baking sheet, and cover well. Bake at 350°F
     for 30 minutes. Turn off oven and leave steaks in closed hot
     oven up to one hour, until ready to serve.

5   **Prepare crispy onions:** Separate sliced onions into rings.
     Dredge onion rings in potato starch. Heat oil in skillet or
     saucepan. Fry onion rings in hot oil until crispy.

6   **To serve:** Place each mini kugel in center of a dinner plate.
     Place steak on top, and top with crispy onions.

This roast is fabulous! The balsamic vinegar locks in the juices, giving it a delicious flavor.
This dish pairs well with a semi-dry white wine.

BALSAMIC FRENCH ROAST

MEAT . YIELDS 10-12 SERVINGS

1 (5-pound) French roast	DRESSING
2 Tablespoons oil	1 cup dark brown sugar
1 onion, diced	1 cup ketchup
2 cloves garlic, crushed	1 cup water
	¾ cup balsamic vinegar
	2 teaspoons apricot jam

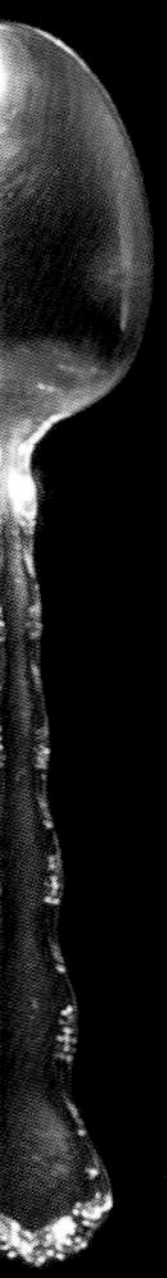

1 **Preheat oven to 350°F.**

2 **Combine oil and onions in a roasting pan. Place in oven; bake for 25 minutes, until onions are soft. Remove from oven.**

3 **Use an immersion blender to combine dressing ingredients in a small bowl.**

4 **Rub roast with garlic. Place in roasting pan over onions. Pour dressing over roast and cover pan tightly.**

5 **Bake for 3 hours.**

For a great variation of this roast, make crepes (see Perfect
Pesach Lukshen, page 48) and fill with pulled brisket.
Spoon mushroom sauce over it and voila!
You have an elegant appetizer!

PULLED BRISKET

MEAT . YIELDS 6-8 SERVINGS

A roast with a bang!

The recipe instructions include cooking the sauce, but if you are short on time you can just blend the sauce ingredients, and that also works well.

1   (3-4 pound) second cut brisket

1   Tablespoon prepared horseradish

1   Tablespoon imitation mustard

½-1   cup ketchup, to taste

1   cup water

2   teaspoons garlic, chopped

¼   cup brown sugar

¼   cup vinegar

salt, to taste

pepper, to taste

1   Preheat oven to 425°F.

2   Place brisket into roasting pan.

3   Combine remaining ingredients in a 4-quart saucepan and cook over low heat for 10 minutes, stirring occasionally.

4   Pour sauce over meat in pan. Cover and seal pan tightly. Bake for 15 minutes.

5   Reduce oven temperature to 200°F. Bake overnight or at least 6 hours. Remove pan from oven and set aside until cool enough to handle. Wearing disposable gloves if desired, remove fat from meat and discard.

6   Use two forks to shred the meat. Rewarm in sauce.

This dish just begs to be noshed on — preferably with matzo.

FLANKEN WITH SWEET POTATOES

MEAT . YIELDS 3 GENEROUS SERVINGS

4   large sweet potatoes

½   cup brown sugar

1 ½   teaspoons cinnamon

3   large strips flanken

    salt, to taste

    pepper, to taste

1   teaspoon nutmeg, or to taste

1 Cut sweet potatoes into spears (not rounds). Liberally sprinkle with brown sugar and cinnamon. Place into a roasting pan.

2 Place flanken over sweet potatoes and sprinkle with salt, pepper, and nutmeg to taste.

3 Bake, tightly covered, at 350°F for 3-4 hours until meat is tender.

A homey comfort food that your teenage boys will adore. This is a chef's favorite that comes with a built-in side dish. Finger-lickin' good — don't count on having any left over! Don't skip the nutmeg; it adds a unique flavor.

My cousin, who is very innovative in the kitchen, recommended this brisket recipe. Our photographer asked to take a break after photographing it, because it looked so good, he wanted to try some. He gave it two enthusiastic thumbs up!

BABY BELLA AND CRANBERRY BRISKET

MEAT . YIELDS 10 SERVINGS

1 (4-pound) brisket	
1 cup chicken broth	
1 cup jellied cranberry sauce	
¼ cup potato starch	
1 large onion, sliced	
4 cloves garlic, chopped	
¾ Tablespoon dried rosemary	
salt, to taste	
pepper, to taste	
12 ounces baby Portobello mushrooms, cleaned and halved	

1 Preheat oven to 400°F.

2 Whisk together broth, cranberry sauce, and potato starch.

3 Pour mixture into a large roasting pan. Add onions, garlic, and rosemary.

4 Season roast with salt and pepper. Place over onions in roasting pan. Spoon cranberry mixture in the pan over the meat.

5 Cover. Bake for 2½ hours.

6 Add mushrooms and bake, covered, for additional 45 minutes.

7 Cool. Slice thinly across the grain.

8 Reheat in sauce before serving.

The best way to cook a standing rib roast is to use a spice rub, cook on a high temperature to medium-rare, and serve it fresh. Since this does not lend itself well to Yom Tov-style cooking, we developed this recipe, which got rave reviews.

STANDING RIB ROAST

MEAT . YIELDS 6-8 SERVINGS

1	(3-4 bone) standing rib roast
4	Tablespoons olive oil
4	onions, diced
3	cloves garlic, crushed
1 ½	cups dry red wine

BASTING MIXTURE

2	Tablespoons onion soup mix (or use spice mix in the note on page 108)
2	Tablespoons tomato paste
2	Tablespoons brown sugar
¼	cup water

1 Preheat oven to 500°F.

2 Heat olive oil in a 12″ skillet. Add onions and garlic. Sauté until translucent.

3 Place sautéed onions and garlic into a roasting pan. Add roast to pan. Pour red wine over roast.

4 Cover and bake 30 minutes.

5 Combine basting ingredients in a small bowl. Remove roast from oven and spoon mixture over. Cover roast again.

6 Reduce heat to 325°F. Bake 2½-3 hours.

SPINACH-STUFFED MINUTE STEAK

MEAT . YIELDS 6 SERVINGS

1 (3-pound) minute steak roast (deveined) OR boneless brisket, ½-inch thick

2 Tablespoons olive oil

1 large onion, sliced into rounds

½ pound Portobello mushrooms

4 cloves garlic, chopped

1 (16-ounce) bag frozen spinach, thawed and drained

salt, to taste

½ teaspoon pepper, plus more to rub on steak

1 cup prepared mashed potatoes

kitchen twine

1 Preheat oven to 425°F.

2 Heat olive oil in a skillet. Add onions and mushrooms and sauté until tender. Add garlic. Stir in spinach, salt, and pepper. Cook for 2 minutes, then remove from heat. Combine with mashed potatoes; set aside to cool.

3 Place meat on work surface. Place filling along one end of meat. Roll up as tightly as possible around filling. Tie rolled meat with kitchen twine. Place into roasting pan, seam side down. Rub salt and pepper into surface of meat.

4 Cover and bake for 25 minutes.

5 Uncover and bake for an additional 25 minutes.

6 This meat is best prepared fresh. If you freeze the cooked steak, defrost overnight in fridge and reheat in oven at 300°F, covered, until just heated through (20-30 minutes). Do not over-bake or steak will dry out.

One Chol HaMoed Succos, I ate this at a friend's house. I had barely finished my portion before I was deep into discussion on how this recipe can be modified to a Pesach version. Use extra stuffing as a side dish.

Even though this roast has many steps, each step is simple. The end result is a tasty, melt-in-your-mouth, soft roast. If you like to slice your roast cold, do so before the second baking the next day.

SOFT AND SAVORY FRENCH ROAST

MEAT . YIELDS 12 SERVINGS

2 Tablespoons oil	salt, to taste
2 onions, cut into chunks	pepper, to taste
1 carrot, cut into chunks	1 (15-ounce) can tomato sauce
1 beef tomato, cut into chunks	2 Tablespoons chicken consommé powder
½ red bell pepper, cut into chunks	1 (5-pound) French roast
2 cloves garlic, sliced	1 cup red wine
paprika, to taste	

1 Heat oil in an 8-quart pot. Add onions, carrot, tomato, red pepper, and garlic. Sauté until tender. Add paprika, salt, and pepper. Sauté a few minutes longer. Add tomato sauce and chicken consommé powder; stir to combine.

2 Place roast into pot. Cover. Cook 2 hours over low heat. Check occasionally and, if most of the liquid has evaporated, add water.

3 Add wine. Cook for an additional hour.

4 Remove roast from pot, leaving gravy, and place into a large roasting pan. Blend gravy in pot with an immersion blender until almost smooth, leaving some texture. Pour gravy over roast in pan.

5 Cover and refrigerate overnight. Roast may be frozen at this point. If frozen, defrost in refrigerator before baking (Step 6).

6 The next day, bake at 275°F for 4 hours.

SIDES

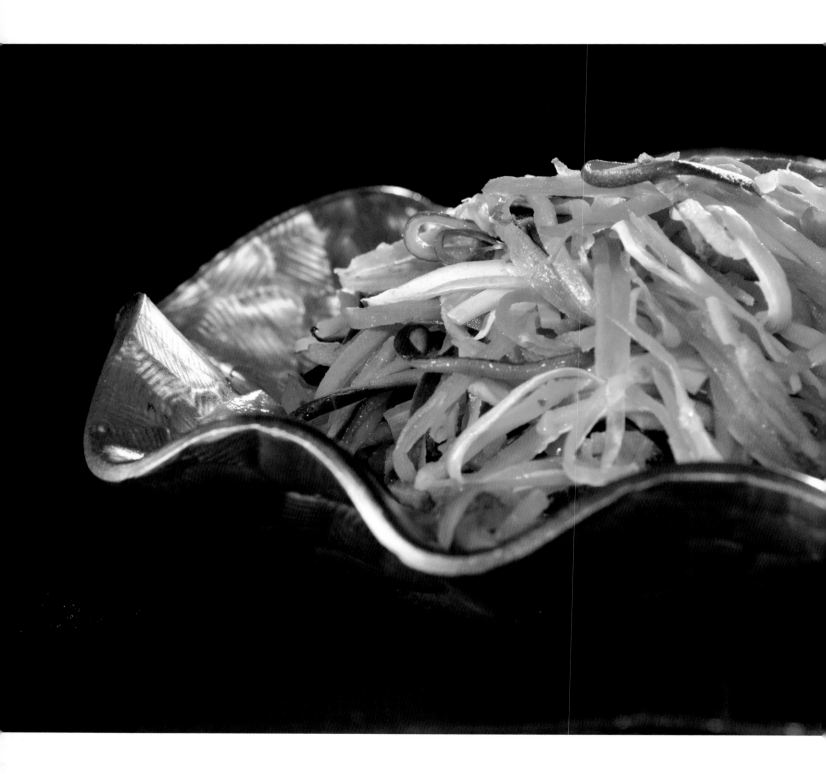

This recipe was inspired by a recent Sheva Berachos I attended. The julienned vegetables added a burst of color and flavor to the main dish. I promptly went out to buy a julienne peeler and started to experiment. The key is to cook the vegetables just long enough to be tender. For optimal results, this should be served fresh.

VEGETABLE JULIENNE

PAREVE . YIELDS 6 SERVINGS

1   carrot

½   medium sweet potato

1   zucchini, unpeeled

1   yellow squash, unpeeled

1   Tablespoon olive oil

1   small onion

1   stalk celery, diced

1   teaspoon salt

2   cubes frozen parsley

1   Using a julienne peeler, or with a knife, julienne carrot, sweet potato, and squashes. When julienning squash, stop when you reach the seeds. Discard seeds (or use for another dish). Cut onion into narrow strips.

2   Heat oil in a large skillet and sauté onion until translucent, 7-8 minutes. Add julienned vegetables, celery, salt, and parsley to skillet and sauté over medium heat for 7-9 minutes. Vegetables should be tender, not soft or mushy. Serve hot.

AUTUMN-HUED VEGETABLES

PAREVE . YIELDS 10 SERVINGS

2 large beets

1 medium butternut squash, peeled and cut into 1-inch cubes

1 (10-ounce) bag pearl onions, peeled

1 teaspoon salt, divided, plus more for sprinkling

½ teaspoon black pepper, divided

1 pint container grape tomatoes

1 bag chestnuts, halved

olive oil

1 **To roast beets:** Preheat oven to 400°F. Scrub the beets thoroughly , then wrap them loosely in aluminum foil. Place the wrapped beets onto a baking sheet and roast for 50-60 minutes. Let the beets cool enough to handle. Hold one of the beets in a paper towel and use the edges of the paper to rub the skin away. The skin should peel away easily; if it doesn't, the beets likely need to cook for a little longer. Peel both beets.

Steps 2 and 3 can be done at the same time as beets:

2 Grease a baking sheet well with nonstick cooking spray. Place butternut squash and pearl onions on prepared baking sheet. Drizzle with olive oil; sprinkle with ½ teaspoon salt and ¼ teaspoon black pepper. Place in oven and bake 40 minutes.

3 Grease a second baking sheet well with nonstick cooking spray. Place grape tomatoes and chestnuts on prepared baking sheet. Drizzle with olive oil; sprinkle with ½ teaspoon salt and ¼ teaspoon black pepper. Place in oven and bake 20 minutes.

4 Dice roasted beets. Toss all vegetables; immediately before serving drizzle with a little bit of olive oil and sprinkle with salt. Serve while still warm. These vegetables can also be served at room temperature but allow the vegetables to cool in a single layer uncovered so that they stay tender.

As I was eating this at a Bar Mitzvah, I phoned a fellow cookbook team member and said, "I just ate a new recipe for our book!" Here it is!

SKEWERED VEGETABLES

For a meat meal, add chicken or beef cubes to the skewer, just increase baking time.

PAREVE . YIELDS 6 SERVINGS

3   bell peppers, various colors, cut into 1-inch cubes

1   box cherry tomatoes

1   yellow squash, unpeeled, cut into 1-inch cubes

1   zucchini squash, unpeeled, cut into 1-inch cubes

1   box fresh mushrooms, cleaned

DRESSING

1   Tablespoon brown sugar

1   Tablespoon vinegar

½   teaspoon salt

⅛   teaspoon black pepper

⅛   teaspoon cinnamon

1   teaspoon dried basil

3   Tablespoons olive oil

1   Preheat oven to 425°F. Line 2 baking sheets with parchment paper.

2   **Prepare the dressing:** In a small jar, combine dressing ingredients and shake well.

3   Thread vegetables onto short wooden skewers, alternating types of vegetables and color of peppers.

4   Place skewers onto prepared baking sheets. Use a pastry brush to brush with dressing. Bake 40 minutes. (Make sure vegetables do not become too soft and slip off skewers.)

5   For a quick and easy variation, don't thread onto skewers, just bake in single layer on a lined baking sheet.

I store any leftovers in the fridge and then toss with fresh lettuce for a delicious, easy grilled vegetable salad. The flavors in the veggies are bold, so the salad doesn't require any additional dressing.

ROASTED VEGETABLE MEDLEY

PAREVE . YIELDS 8 SERVINGS

6 large Portobello mushroom caps (sliced, optional)

4 bell peppers, various colors, sliced into ½-inch strips

MARINADE

½ cup olive oil

½ cup fresh-squeezed lemon juice

3 cubes frozen garlic

   salt and pepper to taste

DRESSING

¼ cup sugar

⅛ cup vinegar

4 diced scallions

   parsley flakes

1 In a large ziplock bag, or in a large shallow container, combine marinade ingredients. Add mushroom and peppers and marinate for a minimum of 4 hours.

2 Preheat oven to 400°F. Remove vegetables from marinade and spread on a baking sheet or large roasting pan. Roast for 20 minutes, or until tender.

3 **Meanwhile, prepare the dressing:** Combine all dressing ingredients in a small jar or container. Shake or stir to blend.

4 Remove roasted vegetables from oven. Pour dressing over hot vegetables.

5 Serve warm or at room temperature.

(We especially like the potato kugel).

My children look forward to eating this kugel on
Friday afternoon in Bubby's house. Throughout
the long drive to Bubby, this kugel is all they talk
about. Try this recipe once —
I guarantee that you will never make a different
potato kugel recipe. Great for year round too!

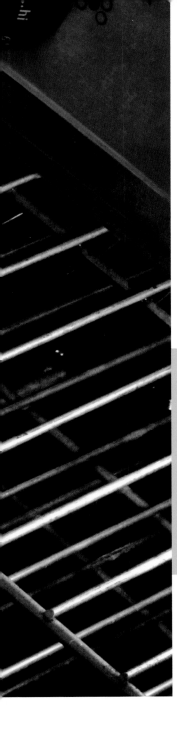

POTATO KUGEL

PAREVE . YIELDS 16-20 SERVINGS

5   pounds Idaho potatoes

1   onion

7   extra-large eggs

⅔   cup oil

1   Tablespoon salt

¼-½   teaspoon white pepper

1   Preheat oven to 550°F. Add oil to a disposable pan and place in the oven to heat. Grease two 8" square pans OR two 9" round pans OR one 9 x 13" pan well.

2   Peel potatoes and place into a large bowl of cold water.

3   In a second large bowl, combine eggs, salt, and pepper.

4   Grate onions and potatoes in the food processor alternately, beginning with onions, then adding potatoes. (The onion reacts with the metal blade and prevents the potatoes from darkening.) Pour potato-onion mixture into egg mixture. Mix well.

5   Carefully remove hot oil from oven and add to potatoes. Stir well. Pour into prepared pans. Bake until the top of the kugel browns, about 25 minutes. Lower temperature to 350°F; bake for an additional ½ hour. Serve hot.

*Colorful and healthy —
an eye-catching low-fat side dish
to enhance your entrée. Feel free
to substitute or add any of your
family's favorite veggies.*

STUFFED ZUCCHINI

PAREVE . YIELDS 8 SERVINGS

4 medium zucchini

1 Tablespoon oil

1 small onion, diced

½ red pepper, diced

½ yellow pepper, diced

½ eggplant, peeled
   and diced

2 eggs

salt, to taste

pepper, to taste

1 Preheat oven to 350°F. Line a baking sheet with parchment paper.

2 Slice zucchini lengthwise and use a spoon to scrape out seeds, leaving enough flesh so that the squash holds its shape. Reserve scraped zucchini flesh. Place zucchini halves, cut side down, onto prepared baking sheet. Bake for 20 minutes.

3 Meanwhile, heat oil in a skillet. Add onion, peppers, eggplant, and reserved zucchini flesh. Sauté until tender.

4 Remove skillet from heat and cool slightly. Add eggs and salt and pepper to taste. Stir well to combine.

5 Remove zucchini halves from oven. Turn the zucchini over and fill cavities with vegetable mixture. Return to oven and bake for an additional 20 minutes.

SMASHED POTATOES

Crispy on the outside, soft on the inside and spiced to perfection. Kid-friendly but adults will love them too.

PAREVE . YIELDS 6 SERVINGS

2 pounds small red potatoes, unpeeled

6 Tablespoons olive oil, divided

salt, to taste

pepper, to taste

garlic powder, to taste

paprika, to taste

1 Scrub potatoes and place into a large pot with water to cover. Bring to a boil and cook until easily pierced with fork, 15-20 minutes.

2 Preheat oven to 425°F. Line a baking sheet with parchment paper.

3 Drain the potatoes and dry on a towel or paper towels. Transfer to prepared baking sheet. Drizzle with 3 tablespoons oil and roll potatoes in oil to coat them.

4 Space potatoes evenly on the baking sheet. Cover with a piece of parchment paper and place another baking sheet on top. Press down firmly on top baking sheet, flattening potatoes until ½-inch thick.

5 Sprinkle with salt, pepper, garlic, and paprika; drizzle with remaining 3 tablespoons oil.

6 Roast potatoes on top rack for 15 minutes, then transfer to bottom rack and continue to roast until well browned, 20-30 minutes longer. Serve immediately.

These are traditional Pesach fare and absolutely scrumptious. Freshly fried, room temperature, or brought along on a Chol HaMoed trip — no matter how many chremslach I make, I never have enough.

CHREMSLACH

PAREVE . YIELDS 18 SERVINGS

6 potatoes, peeled and cut into large chunks

6 eggs

salt, to taste

pepper, to taste

½ cup oil, for frying

1 Place potatoes into a large pot and add water to cover. Bring to a boil over medium-high heat. Cook until soft, about 30 minutes.

2 Drain. Cool until easy to handle. Mash potatoes; combine with remaining ingredients.

3 In a deep skillet over medium-high heat, heat oil. Use a tablespoon to drop potato mixture into hot oil, leaving 1 inch between spoonfuls. Do not crowd pan. Fry until medium brown. Flip to brown on other side. Drain on paper towels. Best eaten immediately.

When I shared the recipes of the Pesach
cookbook with my mother she laughed
out loud. When I asked what was so
funny, she said that she does not use most
of the featured ingredients on Pesach so
she would save it for year-round use.
Ma, this one is for you!

Dear Crew!
Georgeous, as usual—
keep up the good work—
אהבה רבה
"Mommy!"

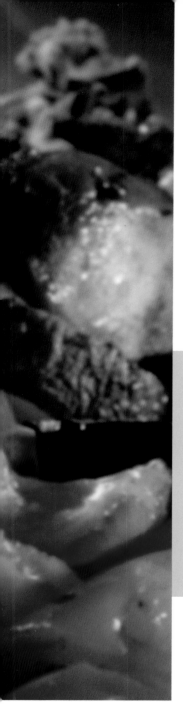

FLANKEN-POTATO KUGEL

MEAT . YIELDS 12 SERVINGS

6 large Idaho potatoes

1 onion

4 eggs

1½ teaspoons salt

¼ teaspoon pepper

⅓ cup oil

1 pound boneless flanken, cut into chunks

1 Using a food processor fitted with the fine grater blade or the S-blade, shred potatoes and onion. Transfer to large bowl. Add eggs, salt, and pepper. Mix until smooth.

2 Pour oil to make a thin layer on the bottom of a 9 x 13" pan. Pour half of potato mixture into pan. Layer with flanken and remaining potato mixture.

3 BAKING OPTIONS

1. Preheat oven to 425°F. Bake 2 hours, uncovered.

2. Preheat oven to 500°F and bake for ½ hour, uncovered. Lower oven to 200°F. Set a pan of water on rack underneath kugel to keep moist. Cover kugel well and bake overnight.

3. Layer potatoes and meat in a slow cooker; bake on HIGH for 4-5 hours, and then reduce to LOW; cook several additional hours until ready to serve.

SPINACH KUGELETTES

PAREVE . YIELDS 6-8 SERVINGS

16	ounces frozen chopped spinach, thawed and drained	2	eggs
2	Tablespoons oil	1	Tablespoon potato starch
2	onions, diced	1	teaspoon salt
2	Tablespoons mayonnaise	¼	teaspoon garlic powder
2	Tablespoons water	¼	teaspoon onion powder

1 Preheat oven to 350°F. Lightly grease a muffin tin OR a 9" round pan.

2 Heat oil in a large skillet. Add onions and sauté until translucent.

3 Discard any liquid that drained from spinach. Add spinach to onions and cook 15 minutes. Remove from heat.

4 Cool slightly; add mayonnaise and water. Beat eggs in a small bowl, then add to skillet, stirring constantly so the eggs don't curdle. Add remaining ingredients.

5 Divide mixture evenly among cups of prepared muffin pan or spread mixture in prepared 9" pan.

6 Bake 35 minutes for kugelettes and 45 minutes for kugel.

I called my friend Nechama in Israel, a great cook who has made Pesach for the past 15 years, and asked for her favorite recipe. She told me that her best Pesach recipe is an apple crisp from her good friend Ahuva in Cincinnati. I called Ahuva who gave me the number of Elisheva in Edison who shared this recipe.

STRAWBERRY APPLE CRISP

PAREVE . YIELDS 12 SERVINGS

7	Granny Smith apples, peeled and diced
½	bag (8 ounces) frozen strawberries, thawed and sliced
½	cup sugar
2	teaspoons lemon juice
½	teaspoon cinnamon

CRUMB TOPPING

2½	cups potato starch
1	cup sugar
1	egg
1	cup oil
4	ounces ground walnuts

1   In a 10-inch round Pyrex baking dish, layer diced apples and sliced strawberries. Sprinkle with sugar, lemon juice, and cinnamon. Toss gently.

2   In a bowl, use a fork or your hand to combine topping ingredients, until the mixture resembles coarse crumbs. Sprinkle onto apple/strawberry mixture to coat.

3   Bake at 350°F for 1 hour.

I really like mushrooms so don't take my word for it … but I don't think I was the only one sneaking bites of this kugel! A great kugel that can be made all year round.

MUSHROOM KUGEL

PAREVE . YIELDS 10 SERVINGS

2 large red onions, sliced

3 Tablespoons oil

2 pounds mushrooms, peeled and sliced

3 eggs

½ cup mayonnaise

2 Tablespoons potato starch

2 Tablespoons onion soup mix

garlic powder, to taste (about ¼ teaspoon)

pepper, to taste

1 Preheat oven to 350°F. Coat a 9-inch round baking pan with nonstick cooking spray.

2 Heat oil in a skillet and sauté onions till soft, about 8 minutes.

3 Add mushrooms and sauté for an additional 2 minutes.

4 In a large bowl, combine mushroom-onion mixture with remaining ingredients. Stir well to combine.

5 Pour mixture into prepared pan. Bake for 45–60 minutes, until top is browned.

GRILLED VEGETABLES

PAREVE . YIELDS 10 SERVINGS

1 eggplant, unpeeled

coarse salt, for sprinkling

1 zucchini, unpeeled

1 yellow squash, unpeeled

3 plum tomatoes,
cut into ½-inch wedges

3 Portobello mushroom
caps, sliced

20 small pearl onions, peeled

½ red pepper, cut into strips

½ yellow pepper, cut into
strips

salt, to taste

MARINADE

½ cup olive oil

½ cup balsamic vinegar

4 cloves garlic, crushed

1 Cut eggplant into 2-inch chunks, then into strips. To remove bitterness, place on paper towels on a flat surface, skin side down. Sprinkle with coarse salt, and let sit for about 20 minutes. Rinse and pat dry.

2 Cut squash into strips about the same size as the eggplant.

3 Place all vegetables into a large ziplock bag. In a small bowl, combine marinade ingredients. Pour marinade over vegetables in bag and gently shake to coat. Marinate in refrigerator overnight (or at least a few hours).

4 Line a baking sheet with parchment paper. Drain marinade from bag. Place all vegetables onto a prepared baking sheet, skin side up, and sprinkle with salt. Bake at 425°F for 45 minutes.

This recipe is very versatile. You can vary the vegetables and their quantities according to your own taste.

Beautiful and healthy!
For a more interesting effect, try skewering the
vegetables before grilling and serve as kabobs.
If you have leftovers, toss with greens and add
your favorite dressing for a hearty salad.

My father is on a strict diet. My mother invented this recipe to replace the high-calorie salt and pepper kugel he loves. We took it one step further and created a sweet version.

"LUKSHEN" KUGEL — TWO WAYS

PAREVE . YIELDS 9-12 SERVINGS

SALT AND PEPPER KUGEL

- 1 spaghetti squash
- ¼ cup mayonnaise
- 2 eggs
- ½ Tablespoon salt
- ½ teaspoon pepper
- 10 ounces frozen chopped broccoli, thawed

SWEET KUGEL

- 1 spaghetti squash
- 1 (20-ounce) can pineapple tidbits, drained well
- 2 eggs
- ½ cup oil
- ¼ cup sugar
- 1 teaspoon cinnamon

1 Preheat oven to 425°F.

2 Line a baking sheet with parchment paper. Place whole spaghetti squash onto prepared baking sheet and roast for ½ hour.

3 Remove squash from oven. Cool slightly. Cut in half; discard seeds. Over a large bowl, using a fork, scrape down the insides of squash to make spaghetti-like strings.

4 To the bowl, add ingredients of kugel you wish to make. Stir well to combine. Drain excess liquid.

5 Coat an 8" square baking pan with nonstick cooking spray. Pour mixture into pan. Bake until golden brown, about 1 hour.

CALIFORNIA MIX VEGETABLE KUGEL

PAREVE . YIELDS 6-8 SERVINGS

1 (16-ounce) bag California mix frozen vegetables (broccoli, cauliflower, carrots)

1 Tablespoon oil

1 small onion, diced

¼ cup mayonnaise

¼ cup coffee whitener (optional)

2 Tablespoons potato starch

1 egg

salt, to taste

pepper, to taste

1 Preheat oven to 350°F. Place frozen vegetables into a 6-quart pot with just enough water to cover. Cook over medium-high heat until very soft, about 45 minutes. Drain and mash the vegetables. (You can save the cooking water for use in soups as vegetable stock.)

2 Meanwhile, heat oil in saucepan. Add onion; sauté until translucent. Add remaining ingredients. Combine with mashed vegetables. Mix well.

3 Pour into an 9″ square pan. Bake 1 hour, till lightly browned.

When you get tired of peeling, try this kugel. You will be delighted to be done in 10 minutes with minimal cleanup. Double the recipe for a 9 x 13″ pan.

WHIPPED POTATOES
WITH BASIL

A twist on the regular Pesach potato parade. The basil gives it a beautiful hue and adds a fresh herbal taste.

MEAT/PAREVE . YIELDS 6 SERVINGS

2	pounds large Yukon Gold OR white boiling potatoes
1	teaspoon salt
6	cubes frozen basil
½	cup chicken stock OR ½ cup water combined with ½ teaspoon chicken consommé powder
2	teaspoons salt
1	teaspoon pepper

1 Peel potatoes, cut into chunks, and place into a large pot. Add water to cover. Add salt and bring to boil. Cook for 20-25 minutes, until very tender. Drain well in a colander. Return potatoes to saucepan; steam, uncovered, over low heat until any remaining water evaporates.

2 Using a handheld mixer with a beater attachment, beat the hot potatoes in the pot until they are broken up. Add the basil, chicken stock, salt, and pepper and beat until smooth. Serve hot.

I prepared this one erev Shabbos when my sister-in-law was coming for the weekend. As we cooked together on Friday, we schmoozed and absent-mindedly kept noshing on these vegetables right out of the pan. By the time we reached the main course on Friday night there were just a few pieces left to serve!

ROASTED ROOT VEGETABLES

PAREVE . YIELDS 10-12 SERVINGS

2	parsnips
2	large carrots
2	turnips
2	sweet potatoes
2	Yukon Gold potatoes
3	Tablespoons olive oil
	salt, to taste
	pepper, to taste

1 Preheat oven to 425°F. Line a baking sheet with parchment paper.

2 Peel all vegetables and cut into sticks.

3 Place in a single layer on prepared baking sheet.

4 Brush with olive oil; sprinkle with salt and pepper.

5 Bake for 45 minutes-1 hour.

To make grilled asparagus as shown, trim lower ends from white asparagus spears and place on a baking sheet lined with parchment paper. Drizzle with olive oil, salt, pepper and paprika. Roast at 425°F for 25 minutes.

POTATO-MEAT KUGEL

MEAT . YIELDS 20 SERVINGS

MEAT LAYER

- 4 Tablespoons oil
- 1 large onion, diced
- 1 pound ground beef
- 8 Tablespoons ketchup
- 2 teaspoons brown sugar
   salt, to taste
   pepper, to taste

POTATO LAYER

- 5 pounds Idaho potatoes
- 8 eggs
- ¾ cup oil
- 1 heaping Tablespoon salt

1 Preheat oven to 375°F. Grease a 9 x 13" pan well.

2 **Prepare meat layer:** Heat oil in 10-inch skillet over medium heat. Add onion and sauté 5 minutes. Add ground beef to onions and sauté, stirring frequently and breaking up with the spoon, until meat is browned. Add ketchup, brown sugar, salt, and pepper. Mix well. Remove from heat.

3 **Prepare potato layer:** Peel potatoes and cut into chunks. Keep in cold water until ready to use. Using a food processer fitted with the S-blade, process the potatoes until they are chopped but not puréed. There may be some bigger pieces left. If your food processor doesn't hold all 5 pounds, do this step in batches. Transfer processed potatoes to a bowl; add eggs, oil, and salt. Mix well.

4 Pour half the potato mixture into prepared pan. Carefully spoon meat mixture over potato mixture; spread meat evenly over potatoes. Pour remaining potato mixture over the meat, spreading to cover the surface.

5 Bake, uncovered, 1½ hours or until done.

I used to be a terrible potato kugel chef. My kids would not eat my kugel, so I started buying it at my local take-out. One Friday I called my sister to vent that my kids would not touch my potato kugel. She gave me this foolproof recipe. However, if your potato kugel is a favorite, by all means use it.

This is one of those absolutely perfect recipes. All you need to do is follow the instructions to a T and the results will be amazing. Pleasing to the eye and utterly delicious. If you don't care to roll, layer the vegetables in a 9 x 13" aluminum pan.

VEGGIE ROLL-UP

PAREVE . YIELDS 16-20 SERVINGS

2 large sweet potatoes, peeled

3 white potatoes, peeled

2 large carrots, peeled

3 zucchini squash, unpeeled and scrubbed

2 onions

1 small red pepper, seeds discarded

handful of fresh checked parsley OR dill, optional

salt, to taste

pepper, to taste

4 eggs

½ cup potato starch

½ cup oil

2 Tablespoons chicken consommé powder

1 Preheat oven to 350°F. Line a baking sheet with parchment paper.

2 Using a food processor, slice all vegetables thinly. Add remaining ingredients to a large bowl. Add sliced vegetables and stir well to combine.

3 Pour mixture onto prepared pan and smooth so mixture is evenly distributed.

4 Bake, uncovered, for one hour and 45 minutes. Remove from oven.

5 When cool enough to handle, roll jelly roll-style, using the parchment paper to help you roll. Wrap tightly in foil and freeze. Slice when partially frozen. Reheat covered.

Thank you once again for your cookbook. We made a פלאנקן on Yom Tov + served onion chicken from Bk#4. roast a veg. roll from this years book

After photographing this kugel, I took a sliver to taste. Not bad, I thought. But as the photo session continued I found myself going back again and again for "tastes." Then I noticed that I wasn't the only one sneaking pieces out of the pan. By the time we had finished photographing, the pan was cleaned to the bottom!

CABBAGE KUGEL

PAREVE . YIELDS 20 SERVINGS

2	Tablespoons oil	½	teaspoon pepper
3	onions, diced	¼	cup sugar, or to taste
2	(1 pound) bags shredded green cabbage	6	eggs, separated
1	Tablespoon salt	⅓	cup potato starch

1 Preheat oven to 350°F. Coat one 9 x 13" or two 9" round pans with nonstick cooking spray.

2 In a large skillet, heat oil. Sauté onions until light brown. Add cabbage. Cover the skillet and cook, stirring occasionally, until cabbage is wilted. Add salt, pepper, and sugar. Stir to combine.

3 Remove from heat and add egg yolks, stirring rapidly while adding, so the eggs don't curdle. Add potato starch.

4 Using an electric mixer, beat egg whites until stiff. Fold into cabbage mixture.

5 Pour into prepared pan(s). Bake for 50 minutes, or until golden.

BUTTERNUT SQUASH KUGEL

PAREVE . YIELDS 24 SERVINGS

4½	pounds butternut squash
¾	cup oil
4	Tablespoons potato starch
1½	cups sugar
1	cup mayonnaise
6	eggs
2	teaspoons vanilla extract
	cinnamon, for sprinkling

1 Preheat oven to 450°F. Line a baking sheet with parchment paper. Lightly grease a 9 x 13" baking pan OR a 10" springform pan. Set aside.

2 Cut squash in half lengthwise. Scoop out seeds and discard. Place squash, cut side down, on prepared baking sheet. Bake for 45 minutes until soft.

3 Lower oven temperature to 350°F.

4 Scoop out squash flesh and place into a large bowl. Add oil, potato starch, sugar, mayonnaise, eggs, and vanilla. Stir well to combine. Pour batter into prepared pan. Sprinkle top with cinnamon.

5 Bake for 1 hour.

DESSERT

VIENNESE CRUNCH ICE CREAM

PAREVE . YIELDS 20 SCOOPS

6 eggs, separated

4 teaspoons vanilla sugar

1 cup sugar

2 (8-ounce) containers nondairy dessert topping, not whipped

7 Viennese crunch bars, crushed

1 Using an electric mixer, beat eggs whites and sugars until soft peaks form. Cover bowl loosely and refrigerate.

2 Use an electric mixer to whip both containers of topping. Add yolks, beating to combine.

3 Gently fold whites into topping mixture. Gently stir in crushed Viennese crunch bars.

4 Freeze until firm.

Just the name of this dessert gets my stomach rumbling! Not very difficult to prepare, it's every bit as delicious as it sounds. You can purchase ready-made chocolate cups at your local Pesach grocery for an easy and beautiful presentation.

Can't wait to try the Viennese Crunch Ice Cream

My family loves compote. So do I, but I don't love peeling, coring, and slicing apples to make it. This is my "1-2-3 no-fuss compote." (Using frozen rhubarb makes it even easier!)

RHUBARB COMPOTE

PAREVE . YIELDS 12 SERVINGS

2	pounds rhubarb, cut into chunks
1	pound strawberries
1	cup sugar
¼	cup apple juice
1	Tablespoon grated orange zest
½	teaspoon vanilla extract

1 Combine all ingredients except vanilla in a medium pot. Bring to a boil over medium heat, watching carefully that it doesn't bubble over.

2 Turn heat to low and simmer 55 minutes, stirring occasionally and checking to see that it is not burning or sticking to the bottom. Remove from heat and let cool.

3 Stir in vanilla.

4 Serve chilled.

CHOCOLATE MOLTEN CAKE

PAREVE . YIELDS 8 CAKES

4 eggs

1½ cups sugar

4 Tablespoons cocoa

1 Tablespoon vanilla sugar

½ cup potato starch

½ cup ground nuts

¾ cup oil

8 squares Rosemarie pareve chocolate

1 Preheat oven to 350°F. Prepare 8 ramekins on a baking sheet, OR line a cupcake pan with 8 cupcake liners.

2 Using an electric mixer, combine eggs, sugar, and cocoa, beating until thick.

3 Add vanilla sugar, potato starch, ground nuts, and oil. Beat until combined.

4 Pour batter into ramekins or cupcake pan until ⅔ full.

5 Place a square of Rosemarie chocolate in center of each ramekin and then cover chocolate with additional batter, leaving a bit of space for expansion.

6 Bake for 15 minutes. The cake should be just baked, and the center molten chocolate. Serve warm.

I don't know about you, but every time I go out to eat, I find myself skimming the dessert menu hoping they have chocolate molten cake. There is something so delicious about that warm chocolatey melted center that blends so well with vanilla ice cream.

This recipe came from my neighbor, who offered her 16-year old-daughter's services to make it for our photo shoot. Just proves how simple it is to make! I will vouch that it is every bit as sumptuous and delicious as it looks. Thank you, Bruria!

Note: To make the tiramisu dairy, substitute half the dessert topping with cream cheese.

TIRAMISU

PAREVE . YIELDS 20 SERVINGS

1 (8-ounce) box ladyfingers, plus more for garnish

CREAM

1 (16-ounce) container nondairy dessert topping, not whipped

¼ cup confectioners' sugar

1 teaspoon vanilla extract

1 egg

1 egg yolk

¼ cup sugar

2 Tablespoons cocoa

DIPPING MIXTURE

¾ cup hot water

½ cup chocolate liqueur

4 Tablespoons sugar

2 Tablespoons instant coffee granules dissolved in a little hot water

GARNISH

½ (3.5-ounce) bar dark chocolate, shaved, for garnish (optional)

1 **Prepare cream:** In the bowl of an electric mixer, beat topping until stiff. Add confectioners' sugar and vanilla; continue to beat for one minute.

2 In a separate bowl, combine egg, egg yolk, and sugar. Add to topping mixture and beat until combined.

3 Divide cream between 2 bowls. Add cocoa to one bowl, mixing well.

4 Combine dipping mixture ingredients in shallow bowl. Dip ladyfingers in bowl one at a time, so they absorb the flavor.

5 In a trifle bowl, layer as follows:
    dipped ladyfingers
    chocolate cream
    dipped lady fingers
    vanilla cream
Repeat to fill trifle bowl, ending with vanilla cream.

6 Garnish with additional undipped ladyfingers around the rim (see photo). Sprinkle shaved chocolate on top for a finishing touch. Refrigerate until ready to serve.

If you do not have a trifle bowl, or you would like to prepare for individual servings, the tiramisu can be made with fewer layers in a 9 x 13" pan instead. Cut into squares to serve.

STUFFED BAKED APPLE
WITH PECAN SAUCE

PAREVE . YIELDS 6 SERVINGS

6   large Cortland OR Rome Beauty apples

½   cup ground walnuts OR almonds

⅓   cup oil

FILLING

¼   stick (2 Tablespoons) margarine

½   cup chopped walnuts

½   cup chopped filberts

¼   cup sugar

¼   cup brown sugar

½   teaspoon cinnamon

PECAN SAUCE

1   (8-ounce) carton whipped topping, not whipped

½   stick margarine

½   cup brown sugar

1   cup pecans halves

1   Preheat oven to 350°F.

2   Using a melon baller, core apples most of the way through, leaving base intact.

3   Place ground walnuts or almonds into a shallow dish. Using a pastry brush, brush apples with oil; roll oiled apples in nuts. Place apples into 9 x 13" baking pan.

4   Combine filling ingredients and fill apple cavities.

5   Bake for 40-50 minutes, until apples are easily pierced with a fork.

6   **Meanwhile, prepare the pecan sauce:** Beat topping until slightly thickened (NOT until stiff).

7   Over low heat, melt margarine. Add brown sugar and pecans, stirring until combined. Remove from heat. Immediately combine with topping, stirring until smooth.

8   Serve warm with a scoop of vanilla ice cream, or a dollop of additional topping, drizzled with warm Pecan Sauce.

For those of us who are "baking challenged," this is a no-fail dessert that comes out perfect every time.

CHOCOLATE MOUSSE CAKE

PAREVE . YIELDS 10 SERVINGS

8   ounces good quality bittersweet chocolate

1   Tablespoon coffee diluted in ¼ cup hot water

8   eggs, separated

⅔   cup sugar

1   teaspoon vanilla extract

⅛   teaspoon salt

1   Preheat oven to 350°F. Lightly grease a 9" round pan.

2   Melt chocolate in double boiler. Add coffee and mix well. Allow to cool.

3   Using an electric mixer set on high speed, beat egg yolks for 5 minutes. Add sugar, chocolate mixture, vanilla, and salt.

4   In a separate bowl, with clean beaters, beat egg whites until stiff. Gently fold whites into yolk mixture.

5   Pour half the batter into pan. Refrigerate remaining batter.

6   Bake for 25 minutes. Don't overbake. Remove from oven and cool completely.

7   When cake is cool, spread reserved batter over the cake. Freeze until firm. Defrost slightly before cutting into wedges and serving.

A refreshing dessert to end any Yom Tov meal.

Be prepared to bring out seconds!

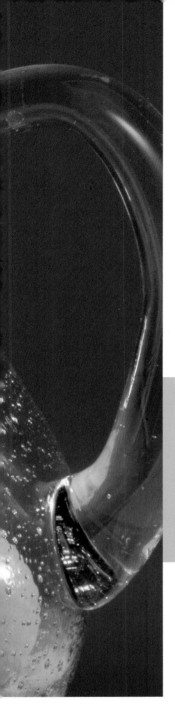

LEMON MOUSSE

PAREVE . YIELDS 12 SERVINGS

6 eggs, separated

1 cup sugar, divided

1 (8-ounce) carton nondairy dessert topping, not whipped

2 lemons

1 Using an electric mixer set on high, beat egg whites with ½ cup sugar until soft peaks form.

2 In a second bowl, beat egg yolks with ½ cup sugar until thick and light yellow.

3 Roll lemons firmly against a hard surface to maximize juice. Cut lemons in half and squeeze juice into a small bowl. Combine unwhipped topping with lemon juice. Add to egg yolk mixture and beat together.

4 Gently fold yolk mixture into beaten egg whites. Pour batter into 9 x 13" pan. Freeze until firm.

This recipe releases most easily from a silicon Bundt pan. To release from a regular Bundt pan, run under cold water for a few minutes. For easier cutting, allow to thaw slightly after unmolding.

TRICOLOR SORBET RING

PAREVE . YIELDS 20 SERVINGS

STRAWBERRY LAYER	MANGO LAYER	KIWI LAYER
1 (1-pound) bag frozen strawberries (no sugar added)	1 (1-pound) bag frozen cut mango	5 fresh kiwis, peeled, cubed, and frozen for 2 hours
1 cup sugar	½ cup sugar	1 cup sugar
1 cup orange juice	1 cup orange juice	

1 **Prepare strawberry layer:** Using a food processor, blend frozen strawberries with sugar and orange juice until smooth. Pour into 9 x 13" OR Bundt pan. Freeze until firm.

2 **Prepare mango layer:** When strawberry layer is firmly frozen, use a food processor to blend mangoes with sugar and orange juice. Pour over strawberry layer in pan. Freeze until firm.

3 **Prepare kiwi layer:** When mango layer is firmly frozen, use a food processor to blend partially frozen kiwis with sugar. Pour over mango layer. Freeze.

4 To serve, cut into slices (bundt pan) or bars (9 x 13" pan).

MINI MOUSSE CUPS

PAREVE . YIELDS 24 SERVINGS

favorite Pesach chocolate
cake recipe
(We recommend the Glazed
Chocolate Cake, page 199.)

2 (16–ounce) containers
nondairy dessert topping,
not whipped

1 (3¼-ounce) box instant
chocolate pudding mix

5 Tablespoons cocoa

6 Tablespoons confectioners'
sugar

6 Tablespoons hazelnut
cream (optional)

shaved chocolate, optional

1 Prepare and bake chocolate cake recipe. Cool cake and
crumble coarsely. Set aside. Reserve some crumbs to top the
mousse cups.

2 Using an electric mixer, whip topping until soft peaks form.
Add confectioners' sugar and continue beating until stiff.
Reserve ⅓ of the topping mixture in the refrigerator.

3 Add pudding, cocoa, confectioners' sugar, and hazelnut cream
(optional) to the remaining topping and beat to combine.

4 **Layer mini mousse cups:** Into each cup, layer crumbled cake,
1 inch chocolate cream, and half-inch topping mixture; top
with reserved cake crumbs or sprinkle with chocolate shavings.

FRUITY COMPOTE

PAREVE . YIELDS 20 SERVINGS

10 large Cortland apples

½ bag frozen strawberries

½ bag frozen rhubarb

½ bag frozen peaches

pomegranate arils (seeds), for garnish

1 Peel and core apples. Cut apples into large chunks and place into an inch of water in a 10-quart pot. Add frozen strawberries, rhubarb, and peaches. Bring to a boil, covered, over medium-high heat.

2 Lower heat; cook for 35-45 minutes, stirring occasionally.

3 When fruit has softened considerably, remove from heat.

4 Using an immersion blender, blend until smooth. Chill.

5 Serve sprinkled with pomegranate arils.

Thank you for another wonderful
cookbook! The Boston creme pie
was a big hit— tasted like *IND*!

This was dropped off the night before the photo shoot and I had to stand guard to make sure that none of my kids (or my husband) took a slice, or even a lick! A spectacular way to wrap up a Yom Tov seudah.

BOSTON CREAM CAKE

PAREVE . YIELDS 16-20 SLICES

8 eggs, separated

1 cup sugar, divided

⅓ cup oil

⅝ cup potato starch

⅓ cup orange juice

1 teaspoon baking powder

1 teaspoon vanilla extract

FILLING

1½ (8-ounce) containers nondairy dessert topping, not whipped

2 (3-ounce) boxes instant vanilla pudding

CHOCOLATE GLAZE

6 Tablespoons hot water

6 Tablespoons oil

6 Tablespoons cocoa

2½ cups confectioners' sugar

1 Preheat oven to 350°F. Prepare two 9" round pans OR one 10 x 15" pan: Line with parchment paper or grease well.

2 Using an electric mixer at high speed, beat egg whites until foamy. Gradually add ½ cup sugar and beat until stiff.

3 In a separate bowl, at high speed, beat yolks with oil and remaining ½ cup sugar for 3 minutes. Add potato starch, orange juice, baking powder, and vanilla; mix to combine.

4 Gently fold yolk mixture into egg whites. Pour into prepared baking pan(s).

5 Bake until golden, about 35 minutes. Cool completely before assembling.

6 **Prepare the filling:** Using an electric mixer at high speed, beat dessert topping until peaks begin to form. Add pudding and continue to beat until combined well.

7 Place one round cake on a serving plate, spread filling on it, and cover with second cake. If using rectangular pan, cut cake in half, spread filling over one half and top with second half.

8 **Prepare the glaze:** Using a fork, mix glaze ingredients in a bowl. Pour glaze over cake. Chill until set.

A delicious classic that presents easily but beautifully. Oh-so-simple to prepare, complement it with a scoop of vanilla ice cream or a dollop of whipped cream. Here we hollowed out the center with a melon baller and filled it with a tiny scoop of ice cream (scooped with the same melon baller). For a finishing touch, we sprinkled it with crushed pistachio nuts.

CLASSIC POACHED PEARS

PAREVE . YIELDS 6-12 SERVINGS

6 Bartlett pears

1½ cups semi-dry red wine

¾ cup sugar

2 Tablespoons lemon juice

2 teaspoons vanilla extract

2 teaspoons cinnamon

1 Peel pears, leaving stem intact. Slice a small sliver from the bottom of each pear so it can stand.

2 Combine remaining ingredients in a medium saucepan. Bring to a boil over medium-high heat, then reduce heat to a simmer. Place pears on their sides in pot and cook for about ½ hour. Turn pears over and cook until soft, about another ½ hour.

3 Carefully remove pears with a slotted spoon and place into a container. Simmer the remaining liquid in the pot until syrupy, about 10 additional minutes. Pour syrup over pears in container.

4 Cover container and cool in refrigerator. Serve chilled. May be served whole, or cut in half as pictured.

RICH CHOCOLATE MOUSSE

PAREVE . YIELDS 20 SERVINGS

14 ounces good-quality dark chocolate

6 eggs, separated

4 teaspoons vanilla sugar

⅓ cup grape juice

1 Using an electric mixer at high speed, beat egg whites until foamy. Gradually add vanilla sugar, beating until soft peaks form. Set aside.

2 Melt chocolate in a double boiler. Set aside.

3 Using a fork, beat yolks with grape juice. Add chocolate to yolks, stirring to blend.

4 Gently fold whites into yolk/chocolate mixture until combined well.

5 Pour batter into 9 x 13" pan, cover, and place in freezer until firm.

6 Remove from freezer 20-30 minutes before serving. Cut into bars or squares. Garnish with fresh fruit, if desired.

When picking dessert for my son's Bar Mitzvah, mousse was one of the choices. I wanted something more exotic, but my husband was adamant that mousse is always a great finale. I deferred to him, and all of our guests scraped their mousse cups clean!

Garnish with various fruits to add some color.

STRAWBERRY "SHORT-CUT"

PAREVE . YIELD: 16 SERVINGS

10 eggs, separated

1 cup sugar, divided

½ cup oil

¾ cup potato starch

1 teaspoon baking powder

1 (3-ounce) box instant vanilla pudding

CREAM

2 (16-ounce) containers frozen nondairy dessert topping, not whipped

1 (3-ounce) box instant vanilla pudding

SAUCE

1 container frozen strawberries with syrup, blended until smooth

1 Preheat oven to 350°F. Lightly grease a 9 x 13" baking pan.

2 Using an electric mixer, beat egg whites until foamy. Gradually add ½ cup sugar and beat until stiff peaks form.

3 In a separate bowl, at high speed, beat yolks with remaining ½ cup sugar until light and creamy. Lower speed to medium and add oil, potato starch, and baking powder. Slowly add pudding and stir until combined.

4 Gently fold egg whites by hand into yolk mixture. Pour into prepared pan. Bake one hour, until a toothpick inserted into center comes out clean.

5 Prepare the cream: Whip dessert topping. Gradually add vanilla pudding; whip until stiffened.

6 When cool, cut cake into slices. Place one slice on a plate, pipe (or spread) cream on top, then place another slice over it and top with more cream. Drizzle sauce generously over all immediately before serving.

For the look of a Neapolitan
Ice Cream, make several
flavors and layer them in the
container.
A classic combination
is chocolate, vanilla and
strawberry.

CANDY ICE CREAM

PAREVE . YIELDS 8-10 SERVINGS

ICE CREAM
4 eggs

1 cup sugar

½ cup oil

1 cup water OR orange juice

BRITTLE
½ cup sugar

3½ ounces pecans, chopped

To make the following flavors, add ingredients to mixture before freezing:

VANILLA
2-3 teaspoons vanilla extract

CHOCOLATE
2.5 ounces good quality bittersweet chocolate, melted.

COFFEE
1 teaspoon coffee dissolved in 1 Tablespoon hot water.

STRAWBERRY
½ bag frozen strawberries, blended until smooth.

---

1 **Prepare the ice cream:** Add ice cream ingredients to a medium pot. Using an immersion blender, blend until smooth. Place over low heat and stir constantly, until the mixture is very hot, but not boiling. Be sure to stir while heating to prevent clumping and curdled eggs. Remove from heat; cool and blend again.

2 **For flavored ice cream:** Prepare ice cream (Step 1). Add optional flavoring ingredients, as desired and mix to combine. Cover and freeze for 6 hours. Remove from freezer and blend again. Store in freezer in an airtight container until ready to serve.

For Candy Ice Cream: Prepare ice cream (Step 1). Cover and freeze for 6 hours. Continue with step 3.

3 **Prepare the brittle:** Line a baking sheet with parchment paper.

- Pour sugar into a very clean pot. (The smallest impurities can allow crystals to form, causing the mixture to seize).

- Cook over medium-low heat, stirring constantly, until all lumps dissolve. Raise heat to medium; cook until sugar melts and turns light brown. If crystals form on the edge of the pan, they can seed crystal formation in the entire mixture and the sugar will seize. Use a pastry brush or paper towel moistened with warm water to brush the sides of the pot very carefully to prevent seizing.

- As soon as sugar has melted and is light brown, remove from heat and add chopped pecans. Pour mixture in a thin layer onto prepared baking sheet. Mixture will harden as it cools, about 10 minutes.

- Use something heavy to break the candied nuts into pieces. Pulse in food processor for a few seconds, reserving some larger pieces for garnish.

4 Remove ice cream from freezer and blend again. Add crushed candy and mix to combine. Garnish with reserved candy pieces.

Note: Even if the mixture seizes and the sugar crystallizes, it still makes for a delicious ice cream!

My neighbor asked me for a gluten-free dessert recipe to make for Shabbos because her parents were coming and they are on a restricted diet. I sent her this roulade, and her mother enjoyed it so much that as soon as Shabbos ended, she called me for the recipe.

CHOCOLATE HAZELNUT ROULADE

PAREVE . YIELDS 15-18 SLICES

4 ounces whole hazelnuts, shelled

4 egg whites

1 cup light brown sugar

1 (16-ounce) container nondairy dessert topping, not whipped

2 (3.5–ounce) bars Rosemarie chocolate

1 Preheat oven to 375°F. Line a baking sheet with parchment paper.

2 Place hazelnuts in a single layer on a second cookie sheet. Toast 8 minutes. Allow to cool. Grind in food processor until fine; be sure not to overprocess or hazelnut butter will result.

3 In the bowl of an electric mixer, beat egg whites until soft peaks form. Add brown sugar. Beat to combine until stiff peaks form. Gently fold in toasted hazelnuts. Spread mixture evenly on prepared baking sheet.

4 Bake for 20 minutes on center rack. Cool. Flip cooled cake over onto a second sheet of parchment paper. Peel parchment paper from baked cake.

5 Whip the topping and divide into 2 bowls.

6 Melt Rosemarie chocolate in double boiler and allow to cool slightly. Set aside 2 tablespoons melted chocolate, and fold remaining melted chocolate into one of the bowls of whip.

7 **To assemble:** Spread chocolate topping over cake; then spread white topping over chocolate layer. Roll cake, using parchment paper to help you. Drizzle reserved chocolate over the roulade.

CAKE & COOKIES

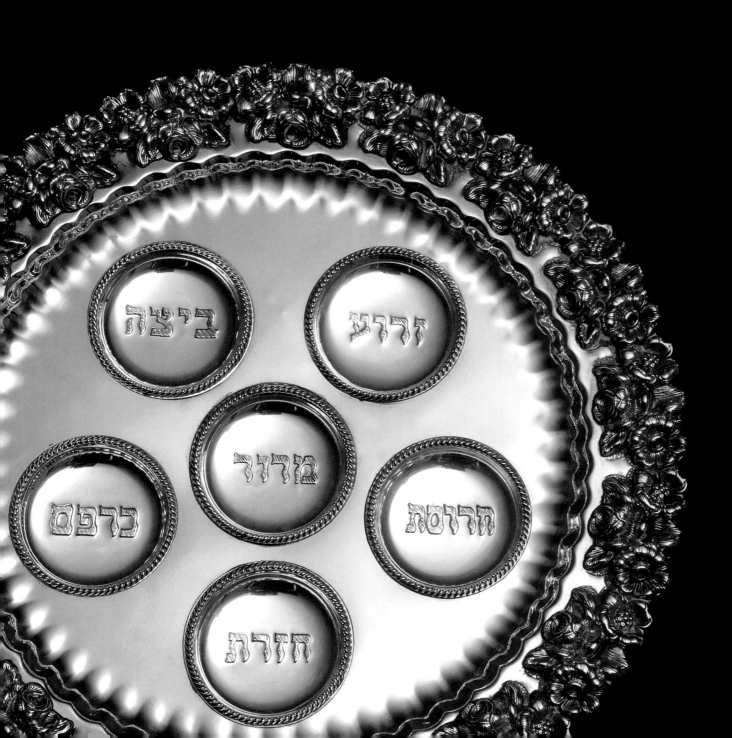

GLAZED CHOCOLATE CAKE

PAREVE . YIELDS 15-20 SERVINGS

5 eggs

1½ cups sugar

1 teaspoon vanilla sugar

1 cup oil

1 teaspoon vanilla extract

½ cup cocoa

pinch instant coffee

¾ cup potato starch

1 teaspoon baking soda

1 teaspoon vinegar

GLAZE

1 cup confectioners' sugar (or more, as needed)

3 Tablespoons hot water

3 Tablespoons cocoa

3 teaspoons oil

1 Preheat oven to 350°F. Lightly grease a 9 x 13" pan.

2 Using an electric mixer, cream eggs, sugars, oil, and vanilla extract in a large mixing bowl until light in color, thickened, and creamy. Add cocoa, coffee, and potato starch.

3 In a small bowl, combine baking soda and vinegar; add to batter. Mix well.

4 Pour batter into prepared pan. Bake for 40 minutes. Allow to cool completely before glazing.

5 When cake is completely cool, in a large bowl, combine glaze ingredients; stir until thick enough to pour. Pour over cake to cover.

To test this recipe, I gave this cake to my neighbor who is on a gluten-free diet. She returned an empty pan two hours later — she couldn't believe that her children had polished it off without even suspecting that it was made without flour!

MANDELBRODT/ BISCOTTI

PAREVE . YIELDS ABOUT 40 PIECES

3 eggs

1 cup sugar

¾ cup oil

1 teaspoon vanilla extract

2 teaspoons baking powder

3½ cups almond flour

½ cup potato starch

8 ounces mini chocolate chips and/or chopped nuts

TOPPING

2 Tablespoons sugar

½ teaspoon cinnamon

Big hits for my family from this year's book were the Biscotti (I made some w/white chips and raisins)

Note: Almond flour can be purchased at a specialty food store or made in the following simple way. Take blanched (peeled) almonds and grind in food processor until very fine. Be careful not to over-process, which will result in almond butter.

1 Preheat oven to 350°F. Line 2 cookie sheets with parchment paper.

2 Using an electric mixer on high speed, beat together eggs and sugar until batter increases in volume, about 7 minutes.

3 Add oil, vanilla, baking powder, and almond flour. Beat until well mixed.

4 Add potato starch a little at a time to form a sticky but workable dough. Add chocolate chips and/or chopped nuts.

5 Using damp hands, form dough into 3 short logs and place horizontally on prepared cookie sheets. Combine sugar and cinnamon in small bowl and sprinkle over logs for topping.

6 Bake 25-30 minutes. Cool and slice into ¾-inch slices. Place slices on their sides on cookie sheets. Bake an additional 10 minutes.

CHOCOLATE CRINKLE COOKIES

PAREVE . YIELDS ABOUT 50 COOKIES

These are so good that we wanted to name them "I Can't Believe It's Pesach Crinkle Cookies," but the title was too long!

¾	cup oil
1¼	cups cocoa plus 1 Tablespoon
2	cups sugar
4	eggs
2	teaspoons vanilla
2	cups potato starch
2	teaspoons baking powder
	confectioners' sugar, for rolling

1 Using an electric mixer, beat together oil, cocoa, and sugar. Add eggs, one at a time, beating to combine. Add vanilla, potato starch, and baking powder. Beat until batter reaches peanut butter consistency.

2 Refrigerate batter, covered, for 1-2 days.

3 Preheat oven to 350°F.

4 Use a small cookie scoop to form balls. Roll each ball in confectioners' sugar. Place onto cookie sheets, 1 inch apart.

5 Bake for 8 minutes — don't over-bake, as cookies will harden as they cool. Cool on cookie sheets for 10 minutes before removing.

This one-bowl recipe is a winner. So simple, just hand the recipe to your kids and you can tackle the "serious stuff"! A quick and easy way to fill the cookie jar.

TOLL HOUSE BARS

PAREVE . YIELDS 48 SQUARES

1½	cups brown sugar
1½	cups sugar
6	eggs
1½	cups oil
4½	teaspoons vanilla sugar
4½	teaspoons baking powder
1½	cups potato starch
7	ounces ground nuts
1	cup chocolate chips

1 Preheat oven to 350°F. Lightly grease two 9 x 13" pans.

2 Using an electric mixer, beat together sugar and eggs until thick and light in color. Add remaining ingredients.

3 Pour batter into prepared pans.

4 Bake for 45 minutes. When cool, cut into 3 x 2" bars.

The chocolate cake and Toll House Bars have graced our Yom Tov table over the past few years, and the pages of "Pesach I" are just about falling apart from use. It is so comforting to have Pesach recipes that are tested and reliable.

My sister became engaged on Pesach,

and we made this cake for the vort.

There was not a crumb left!

MERINGUE LAYER CAKE

PAREVE . YIELDS 12-16 SERVINGS

6 egg whites

¾ cup sugar

8 ounces ground almonds, roasted and cooled

2 (3.5-ounce) bars good quality pareve chocolate (not baking chocolate)

CHOCOLATE CREAM

8 ounces baking chocolate

2 sticks margarine

1 Tablespoon boiling water

1 Tablespoon coffee

½ cup confectioners' sugar

1 Tablespoon vanilla sugar

2 eggs

WHIPPED CREAM LAYER

1 (8-ounce) container nondairy dessert topping, not whipped

1   Preheat oven to 275°F. Line 2 cookie sheets with parchment paper; use a pencil to mark two 7-inch circles on the back of each sheet of parchment paper OR grease four 9″ round pans.

2   Using an electric mixer on high speed, beat egg whites with sugar until stiff peaks form. Fold nuts into egg white mixture.

3   Use a spatula to spread batter over the marked circles, filling them completely OR spread batter in prepared round pans.

4   Bake for 1 hour. Cool completely. Remove from pans; set one meringue aside.

5   Melt good quality pareve chocolate in a double boiler. Pour evenly over the 3 remaining meringue layers.

6   **Prepare the chocolate cream:** In a saucepan over low heat, combine baking chocolate, margarine, water, coffee, confectioners' sugar, and vanilla sugar.

7   Cool somewhat so that eggs won't curdle. Add 2 eggs while stirring constantly. Allow to stand and thicken.

8   Spread chocolate cream evenly over melted chocolate on the 3 meringue layers.

9   **Prepare the whipped cream:** Using an electric mixer, beat defrosted cold topping on high speed. Spread on top of chocolate cream on the 3 layers.

10 Stack layers to assemble cake, ending with reserved meringue. For a more decorative look, reserve some topping and press over top layer through a pastry bag fitted with a large star tip. To serve, cut with a very sharp knife.

CARAMEL CAKE

PAREVE . YIELDS 40 SERVINGS

The ingredients listed make two identical cakes. If your mixing bowl cannot hold this amount of batter, simply halve all of the ingredients listed and make the cake twice.

oil for brushing pan

potato starch for dusting pan

14 egg whites

2 cups sugar

16 ounces ground almonds

CREAM

14 egg yolks

2 cups sugar

1½ cups oil

2 Tablespoons instant coffee, dissolved in 2 teaspoons boiling water

1 Preheat oven to 350°F. Line 2 baking sheets with parchment paper. Brush with oil and sprinkle with potato starch.

2 Using an electric mixer, beat egg whites until soft peaks form. Continue to beat, gradually adding 2 cups sugar.

3 Fold in ground almonds. Divide batter between prepared pans and smooth with a spatula. Bake for 50 minutes. Remove from oven and allow to cool before filling.

4 In a double boiler, mix cream ingredients well. Bring to a boil and let simmer for about 1 hour, stirring occasionally, until thick.

5 When cakes have cooled, layer as follows: cake, cream, cake and then end with cream.

6 Cover well and place into freezer. Cut into squares when frozen. Serve slightly frozen.

Everything I've tried from your booklets has turned out well. I made the caramel cake for my daughter's birthday (7th day of Pesach) this year and it was a wild success. My daughter happened to have looked through the book minutes before I served it and said, "This looks really good..."

Who doesn't enjoy a chewy, chocolately, nutty brownie? Usually, it sits on my counter for nibbling right out of the pan. If you can sneak a pan into the freezer, it makes a pretty dessert presentation; place pan in preheated oven for 5 minutes to warm.

BROWNIES

PAREVE . YIELDS 40 (2-INCH) SERVINGS

3   cups sugar

1   cup + 2 Tablespoons cocoa

¼   teaspoon salt

¼   cup oil

6   eggs

3   cups ground almonds OR filberts

3   teaspoons vanilla extract

    confectioners' sugar, for sprinkling

1   Preheat oven to 350°F. Line a 10 x 16" baking pan with parchment paper.

2   Using an electric mixer, combine all ingredients in a large mixing bowl. Mix until well combined.

3   Spread batter in prepared pan.

4   Bake for 30–45 minutes.

5   Remove from oven and let cool. Cut into squares or rounds (with a lightly greased rim of a glass or cookie cutter). Sprinkle with confectioners' sugar to serve.

We are not sure what makes this cake "Hungarian" or a "brownie," but that's the name it came with, so we stuck with it!

To mimic this fabulous garnish, roast marshmallows on a skewer over a flame. Stack two pieces of cake as pictured and top with the roasted marshmallows. Drizzle with melted chocolate right before serving.

HUNGARIAN BROWNIES

PAREVE . YIELDS 20 BROWNIES

1	cup brown sugar
1	cup sugar
4	eggs
3	teaspoons vanilla extract
1	cup potato starch
1	cup oil
3	teaspoons baking powder
7	ounces ground filberts

1 Preheat oven to 350°F. Line a 9 x 13" pan with parchment paper.

2 Using an electric mixer, on high speed, beat together both sugars and eggs until thick and light in color.

3 On low speed, add remaining ingredients. Pour into prepared pan.

4 Bake 45-50 minutes. Do not over-bake. Cut into squares or bars when cooled.

YODELS

PAREVE . YIELDS 18 YODELS

My friend's son is gluten intolerant. She sends these yodels to each simchah she is invited to so that her son has something special to eat. She makes sure to label them "shehakol" because people constantly mistake them for the real thing! They freeze well.

CAKE

6 eggs, separated

¾ cup sugar, divided

pinch salt

3 teaspoons vanilla sugar

⅓ cup sifted cocoa

FILLING

10 ounces nondairy dessert topping, not whipped

½ (3-ounce) box instant vanilla pudding

GLAZE

1 (8–ounce) bar baking chocolate

1 stick (½ cup) margarine

2 ounces white baking chocolate

1 Preheat oven to 375°F. Line a baking sheet with parchment paper and spray with nonstick cooking spray.

2 Using an electric mixer, beat egg whites with ¼ cup sugar and pinch of salt until stiff.

3 In a separate bowl, beat egg yolks with ½ cup sugar and vanilla sugar until thick and lemon-colored. Add cocoa to yolks and mix until well combined. Gently fold in egg whites mixture.

4 Spread batter onto prepared baking sheet. Bake for 15 minutes. Cool.

5 **Prepare the filling:** Beat topping with the vanilla pudding until stiff.

6 Invert cake onto your work surface. Carefully peel away parchment paper. Spread filling onto cake. Cut the cake vertically into 3 long strips. Roll each strip so that you have three long narrow logs. Cut each log into six 2-inch pieces (18 pieces total). Freeze for at least 2 hours until yodels are frozen.

7 **Prepare the glaze:** Line a baking sheet with parchment paper. Melt baking chocolate and margarine in a double boiler. Stick a skewer or fork into yodels, one at a time, and dip into chocolate to coat. Place coated yodels onto prepared baking sheet.

8 When glaze has set and hardened, melt the white chocolate in a double boiler. Put melted chocolate into a ziplock bag. Cut a small hole in one corner and drizzle chocolate onto each yodel.

9 Keep refrigerated or frozen until ready to serve.

SAVTA CANDY

From Reva's savta, with love! As with most bubbies and savtas, the ingredients are all approximate amounts. This very versatile recipe can easily be adapted to your family's tastes and preferences.

PAREVE . YIELDS 25 PIECES

½ cup ground nuts

1½ cups sugar

1½ cups honey

3 cups assorted whole unsalted nuts, such as cashews, filberts, almonds, and pecans

1 Line a baking sheet with parchment paper. Sprinkle with ground nuts.

2 In a skillet over medium-high heat, combine sugar and honey. Mix well over heat for 5-10 minutes. To test for readiness, take a small spoonful of mixture and drop into a cup of ice water. If it becomes taffy-like, the mixture is ready.

3 Add nuts. Stir to combine. Pour mixture onto prepared baking sheet. Allow to cool. Toffee will harden. Break toffee into pieces.

Mrs. Rochel Weiss of Digestive Wellness in Monsey, NY. shared this wholesome recipe with us. The original recipe was for year-round use; we adapted it for Pesach.

CASHEW BUTTER MUFFINS

PAREVE . YIELDS 30 MUFFINS

10   large eggs, separated

     pinch salt

⅓   cup oil

1   cup honey

1   teaspoon vanilla extract

½   teaspoon ground cinnamon

1½   teaspoons baking soda

2¼   cups cashew butter (18-ounce jar)

1   Tablespoon coffee dissolved in 1 Tablespoon boiling water

1   Preheat oven to 300°F. Line muffin pans with paper liners.

2   Using an electric mixer, beat egg whites on low speed until frothy. Beat in salt; increase speed to high until soft peaks form. Reduce speed to low and add egg yolks, 1 at a time.

3   Slowly add remaining ingredients. Pour batter into prepared muffin pans, filling each cup ⅔ full.

4   Bake for 30 minutes. Remove from pans to cool completely.

SHEHAKOL FREEZER CAKE

PAREVE . YIELDS 24 SERVINGS

NUT LAYER

10 egg whites

1 cup + 1½ Tablespoons sugar

12 ounces ground filberts

CHOCOLATE LAYER

6 ounces good quality bittersweet chocolate

12 egg yolks

1 cup + 1½ Tablespoons sugar

2 sticks (1 cup) margarine

3 teaspoons vanilla sugar

2 Tablespoons coffee, dissolved in 1 Tablespoon hot water

1 Preheat oven to 350°F. Line a 10 x 16" pan OR a baking sheet (for a larger, flatter cake) with parchment paper, or spray with non-stick cooking spray.

2 **Prepare nut layer:** Using an electric mixer, beat egg whites, gradually adding sugar, until soft peaks form. Gently add filberts. Pour into prepared pan. Bake for ½ hour. Remove from oven.

3 **Prepare chocolate layer:** Melt chocolate in a double boiler. Using an electric mixer, beat egg yolks with sugar, margarine, vanilla sugar, and coffee until thickened. Slowly add melted chocolate; mix until combined. Spread over nut layer in pan. Bake for 15 minutes.

4 Remove from oven; cool. Freeze.

5 Cut into squares; serve frozen.

Every family seems to have its own recipe for a shehakol freezer cake. This one is our family's specialty. The smiles on my children's faces tell me it will be passed down in their families, too.

CHOCOLATE ALMOND SOUFFLÉ COOKIES

PAREVE . YIELDS ABOUT 24 COOKIES

My morning coffee partner — these cookies may be the culprits for the extra weight gain over Yom Tov.

6	ounces good quality bittersweet chocolate
3	egg whites
1	Tablespoon vanilla sugar
½	cup sugar
¾	cup chopped roasted almonds

1 Preheat oven to 350°F. Line two cookie sheets with parchment paper.

2 Melt chocolate in a double boiler. Cool slightly. Using an electric mixer, beat egg whites until foamy. Gradually add sugars; beat until stiff peaks form. Fold in melted chocolate and nuts.

3 Drop batter by teaspoons onto cookie sheets, leaving about 2 inches between cookies.

4 Bake for 10-12 minutes. After cookies cool, remove from cookie sheets with a metal spatula. (If cookies are still hot, they will break.)

Perfect for the chocoholic!

FUDGE CHOCOLATE CHIP COOKIES

PAREVE . YIELDS 30 COOKIES

3	cups confectioners' sugar
⅔	cup unsweetened cocoa
⅛	teaspoon salt
1	Tablespoon vanilla extract
2-4	large egg whites, room temperature
1½	cups chocolate chips

1 Preheat oven to 350°F. Line 2 cookie sheets with parchment paper.

2 In a large bowl, combine confectioners' sugar with cocoa and salt. Using a whisk, beat in the vanilla and 2 egg whites.

3 Beat just until the batter is moistened. Batter should be a brownie-like thick and fudgy consistency. If it seems too thick, add a third egg white, and, if needed, a fourth. Stir in the chocolate chips.

4 Scoop the batter by the tablespoon-full onto the prepared cookie sheets. Leave 2 inches between cookies, as they will spread.

5 Bake for 12-14 minutes, until the tops are glossy and lightly cracked.

6 Cool cookies completely on the cookie sheets, then store in an airtight container for up to 3 days.

This is the absolute best Pesach cake I have ever tasted! Even though there are four layers, each one is not difficult, so anyone can look like a "gourmet baker" this Pesach!

My mother, who doesn't use margarine on Pesach, freezes oil overnight to substitute and it works very well.

MILLION DOLLAR CAKE

PAREVE . YIELDS 30 2 ½-INCH SQUARES

CHOCOLATE CAKE

- 6 eggs, separated
- ¾ cup sugar
- ⅓ cup cocoa
- 1 Tablespoon instant coffee, dissolved in 2 Tablespoons warm water
- ½ teaspoon vanilla sugar

1 **Prepare the cake:** Peheat oven to 350°F. Line a baking sheet with parchment paper.

2 Using an electric mixer at high speed, beat egg whites until soft peaks form.

3 In a separate bowl, beat yolks with the rest of the ingredients until thick. Fold into the beaten whites.

4 Pour mixture onto prepared baking sheet. Bake for 15-20 minutes.

COFFEE CREAM
(Don't halve recipe even though it makes a lot!)

- 7 egg whites
- 2 heaping cups sugar
- 3 Tablespoons instant coffee dissolved in ¼ cup warm water
- 4 sticks of margarine OR 2 cups frozen oil

1 **Prepare the coffee cream:** Add egg whites and sugar to a medium pot over low heat, stirring constantly, for 3-5 minutes.

2 Remove from heat and beat very well with an electric mixer, until batter forms a sticky consistency, like marshmallow fluff. Beat in coffee and margarine.

MERINGUE

- 7 egg whites
- 2⅓ cups sugar, divided
- 1 cup ground almonds
- 3 Tablespoons potato starch

1 **Prepare the meringue:** Preheat oven to 275°F. Line 2 baking sheets with parchment paper and grease very well.

2 Using an electric mixer, beat egg whites with ⅓ cup sugar until soft peaks form.

3 Combine almonds with remaining sugar and potato starch. Fold dry ingredients into beaten whites.

4 Divide mixture between prepared pans. Spread batter to cover the pan. Bake 25–30 minutes.

CHOCOLATE CREAM

- 4 eggs
- 1 cup sugar
- 1 Tablespoon instant coffee dissolved in ⅛ cup warm water
- 4 Tablespoons vanilla sugar
- ⅞ cup oil
- ¾ cup cocoa

1 **Prepare the chocolate cream:** Using an electric mixer, combine all ingredients.

2 Refrigerate for ½ hour.

3 **Assemble cake:** Layer cake as follows:

Meringue
Chocolate cream
Chocolate cake
Coffee cream
Meringue
Coffee cream

4 Store in freezer. Use a sharp knife to cut frozen cake.

CHOCOLATE CUPCAKES

PAREVE . YIELDS 24 CUPCAKES

6 eggs

1½ cups sugar

¾ cups potato starch

1½ cups oil

¾ cups cocoa

1½ teaspoons baking soda

FROSTING

1 (1-pound) box confectioners' sugar

1 egg

1 teaspoon vanilla sugar

1 stick margarine

4 Tablespoons cocoa

1 Tablespoon instant coffee dissolved in 2 Tablespoons boiling water

1 Preheat oven to 350°F. Line cupcake pans with cupcake liners, for 24 cupcakes.

2 Using an electric mixer, beat together eggs and sugar until thick and light in color. Lower speed and add remaining ingredients. Beat to combine.

3 Fill cupcake pans two-thirds full of batter. Bake for 15-20 minutes. Remove cupcakes from pan. Cool completely before frosting.

4 **Prepare the frosting:** Using an electric mixer, beat together all frosting ingredients until creamy.

5 Frost cupcakes.

My son has a Pesach birthday and cupcakes are his favorite. Last year I explained to him yet again that cupcakes are not Pesach'dig. What a pleasant surprise to come across this recipe! Yummy and just the thing for kids. I can't wait to see the look on my son's face when I present him with these!

We wanted to include a chocolate chip cookie in our collection. Most cookies we tested were either hard or crumbly. This recipe makes a chewy cookie with a great taste and texture.

CHOCOLATE CHIP DROPS

PAREVE . YIELDS 24 COOKIES

2 eggs

½ teaspoon salt

1 cup sugar

1 teaspoon vanilla extract

3 cups ground filberts

3 (3½-ounce) bars Rosemarie pareve chocolate, cut into "chips" to make 1 ½ cups

1 Preheat oven to 350°F. Grease a cookie sheet or line with parchment paper.

2 Using an electric mixer on high speed, beat together eggs, salt, sugar, and vanilla until thick and light in color. At lower speed, add ground filberts and chocolate pieces.

3 Form batter into walnut-size balls and place on prepared cookie sheet.

4 Bake for 15 minutes. Let cool slightly, 5-7 minutes, before removing from cookie sheet. For really chewy cookies, cover with foil while still warm until completely cooled.

GEBROKTS

EGGPLANT ROLLATINI

MEAT . YIELDS ABOUT 15 ROLLS

A great meat alternative to eggplant parmesan for those with a passion for Italian food.

2 large eggplants

3 eggs

1½ cups matzo meal

½ cup oil, or more as needed for frying

STUFFING

2 Tablespoons oil

2 red onions, thinly sliced

1 pound red cabbage, shredded

3 large carrots, peeled and shredded

1½ pounds ground beef

1 (28-ounce) jar marinara sauce

1 Peel eggplant and cut lengthwise into thin (¼-inch) slices.

2 Beat eggs with a fork in a flat dish. Place matzo meal into second flat dish.

3 Dredge eggplant slices in egg and then in matzo meal.

4 Heat oil over medium-high heat in a large frying pan; fry slices for about 3 minutes on each side until eggplant is softened but coating is not crunchy. Add oil to pan as needed.

5 **Prepare the stuffing:** Heat oil over medium-high heat in a skillet. Add vegetables and sauté until softened, about 8 minutes. Gradually add meat, breaking up large chunks, and continue sautéing until meat is no longer pink.

6 Preheat oven to 350°F. Line a baking pan with parchment paper.

7 Spread 2 tablespoons stuffing over an eggplant slice. Roll up jelly roll style, and place in pan seam side down. Repeat with remaining eggplant and stuffing. Spread marinara sauce over rollups. Bake, uncovered, for about 15 minutes. You may also bake without sauce and warm up sauce to pour over when serving. (Serve extra stuffing, if any, as a side dish.)

Make-ahead tips: You can fry eggplant the day before and store, covered, in the fridge overnight. You can also prepare stuffed rolls and freeze. When ready to use, pour sauce over and bake.

This recipe can easily be doubled and knaidlach can be frozen. To freeze without the balls clumping together, place in a single layer onto a parchment paper-lined baking sheet and freeze. When they are completely frozen, you can place them into a ziplock bag and store in the freezer.

PERFECT KNAIDLACH

PARVE . YIELDS 15 KNAIDLACH

2   eggs

¾   teaspoon salt

    dash white pepper

¼   cup oil

¼   cup water

¾   cup matzo meal

1   Tablespoon chopped parsley (optional)

1   Beat eggs with salt and pepper. Add oil and water. Stir in matzo meal and parsley. Refrigerate mixture for one hour.

2   In a large pot, bring 4 quarts of salted water to a boil. With wet or oiled hands, form walnut-size balls of mixture and drop into boiling water. Cook for 25 minutes, uncovered.

3   Remove cooked balls with slotted spoon. Reheat in soup before serving.

The best Pesach soup accompaniment I have come across yet!

MATZO FARFEL CROUTONS

PAREVE . YIELDS 36 SERVINGS

4	eggs
¼	cup water
	salt, to taste
	pepper, to taste
1	(16-ounce) box matzo farfel OR matzos, crumbled

1 Preheat oven to 400°F. Line a baking sheet with parchment paper.

2 Beat eggs with water, salt, and pepper. Add matzo farfel or crumbled matzos.

3 Bake for 20 minutes, removing often to shake and stir.

4 When cool, break apart any large clumps.

This can also be made with ground beef.

One of our "freezer-friendly" recipes.

VEAL AND EGGPLANT LAYERS

MEAT . YIELDS 9 SERVINGS

2 medium firm eggplants

kosher salt, for sprinkling

2 eggs, lightly beaten

1 cup matzo meal
(to make this non-gebrokts,
substitute with Pesach
crumbs or potato starch)

oil, for frying

VEAL SAUCE

1 pound ground veal

2 Tablespoons oil, divided

1 small onion, chopped

2 (6-ounce) cans tomato
paste

2 cups water

salt, to taste

pepper, to taste

2 Tablespoons sugar

4 cloves garlic, crushed

1 Peel and slice eggplants lengthwise. Place in a single layer on paper towels. Sprinkle with salt. Let stand 15-20 minutes. Rinse and pat dry.

2 **Meanwhile, prepare the veal sauce:** Heat 1 tablespoon oil in a skillet. Add ground veal and stir to break up the meat. Brown until golden. Remove meat from pan, drain drippings and wipe out the pan.

3 Using the same skillet, heat remaining tablespoon of oil. Add onion and sauté until translucent. Remove from heat. Add tomato paste; stir to combine. Slowly add water, stirring constantly until sauce is smooth. Return to medium heat and add salt, pepper, sugar, and garlic. Bring to a boil. Add browned veal and lower heat. Cover and simmer for ½ hour.

4 **Prepare the eggplant:** Heat ¼ cup oil in a deep skillet. Dip eggplant into beaten eggs, then into matzo meal to coat. Fry in oil on each side until golden brown.

5 **Assemble the layers:** Place one layer of fried eggplant into an 8 x 8" pan. Cover with ⅓ of the veal sauce. Repeat layers twice more. Cover and bake at 350°F for 45 minutes. Let stand 15-20 minutes before slicing.

YERUSHALMI KUGEL

PARVE . YIELDS 10 SERVINGS

8 matzos

boiling water, as needed

1 cup sugar, divided

½ cup oil

4 eggs

1½ teaspoons salt

2 teaspoons pepper (or to taste)

1 Preheat oven to 375°F. Grease an 8" round pan.

2 Break matzo into pieces and place into bowl. Pour boiling water over and immediately drain off all the water. Press down on the matzos with pot lid or plate to express as much liquid as possible; drain again. Matzos should not be completely soft.

3 Place ¾ cup sugar and oil into a small saucepan. Cook over medium heat until brown and completely liquefied. Immediately pour over soaked matzos and stir quickly to combine.

4 Beat in eggs and additional ¼ cup sugar, salt, and pepper.

5 Let stand 30 minutes. Pour into prepared pan; bake for 40 minutes or until brown.

Note: Alternatively, this can be fried on both sides in a deep skillet.

The vibrant colors of this kugel add instant eye appeal to any meal ... light, fluffy, and really good.

ZUCCHINI KISHKE KUGEL

PAREVE . YIELDS 20 SERVINGS

KISHKE LAYER

- 2 large carrots
- 1 large potato
- 1 onion
- 1 stalk celery (optional)
- ½ cup oil
- 1 Tablespoon paprika
- 1 teaspoon salt
  dash pepper
- ¾ cup matzo meal
- ⅓ cup potato starch

ZUCCHINI LAYER

- 2 pounds zucchini, unpeeled, cut into chunks
- 2 Tablespoons mayonnaise
- 3 eggs
- 1 Tablespoon onion soup mix (to make your own, see page 108)
  salt, to taste
  pepper, to taste

1 Preheat oven to 350°F.

2 **Prepare kishke layer:** Grate carrots, potato, onion, and celery in the food processor fitted with the S-blade. Transfer to a large bowl. Add oil, paprika, salt, pepper, matzo meal, and potato starch. Mix well.

3 Pour mixture into two loaf pans OR two 8″ round pans OR one 9 x 13″ pan. Bake for 30 minutes. Remove from oven.

4 Raise oven temperature to 375°F.

5 **Prepare the zucchini layer:** While kishke layer is baking, place unpeeled zucchini into a 6 quart pot with water to cover. Cook until soft but not falling apart. Drain well and mash. Add mayonnaise, eggs, and onion soup mix. Add salt and pepper to taste.

6 Pour over kishke layer and bake at 375°F for 45 minutes. Serve hot.

The crumbly crust topped with a deliciously tangy lemon filling makes for a wonderful kosher l'Pesach variation on a classic. Pairs well with tea; a perfect finale to a perfect meal.

For best flavor, use freshly squeezed lemon juice.

LEMON BARS

PAREVE . YIELDS 35 SERVINGS

CRUST

3 sticks margarine,
room temperature

¾ cup confectioners' sugar,
plus more for sprinkling

½ teaspoon salt

2 cups cake meal OR
finely processed matzo meal

1 cup potato starch

FILLING

8 eggs

4 cups sugar

½ cup potato starch

¾ cup lemon juice

1 Preheat oven to 350°F. Line an 11 x 17" baking sheet with parchment paper, or spray with nonstick cooking spray.

2 Using an electric mixer, combine crust ingredients. Press into prepared pan. Bake for 20 minutes.

3 **While crust is baking, prepare the filling:** Using an electric mixer, beat eggs and sugar 7 minutes until light and fluffy; then add potato starch and lemon juice and beat one more minute. Remove baking sheet from oven and pour filling onto baked crust.

4 Return to oven and bake an additional 30 minutes. Remove from oven and refrigerate until cool.

5 Cut cooled cake into squares or logs. Sprinkle with confectioners' sugar before serving.

WISSOTZKY 1849

The exclusive taste of this blend has been
achieved by the ongoing tradition of
searching and blending the world's finest
teas for 150 years. Generations have
consistently preferred
Wissotzky tea.

for quality since 1849

W
WISSOTZKY TEA

My family's Pesach tradition is to eat almost nothing. Chicken and potatoes, with some eggs for variety. So when I married my husband, whose family eats just about any certified "Kosher for Passover" product they can get their hands on, it was a real eye-opener! And they even eat gebrokts! I am slowly but surely acclimating to this new-found way of Pesach, and have even ventured to try a few gebrokts recipes. This one is so good, I gave it to my mother to try after Pesach!

BISCOTTI

PAREVE . YIELDS 30 BISCOTTI

3 eggs

1 cup sugar

1½ cups cake meal OR
finely processed matzo meal

½ cup potato starch

¾ cup oil

½ cup chocolate chips and/or
slivered almonds, craisins, etc.
(optional)

1 teaspoon cinnamon

3 Tablespoons sugar

1 Line a baking sheet with parchment paper.

2 Mix all ingredients to form a very sticky dough. Use your choice of add-ins: chocolate chips, craisins, almonds, etc.

3 Divide dough in half; shape into two logs and place on prepared baking sheet. Bake at 350°F for 20 minutes.

4 Combine cinnamon and sugar in a small bowl.

5 Remove baking sheet from oven. Turn oven to Broil.

6 Cut each log into 1-inch strips. Return strips to cookie sheet, cut sides down. Sprinkle with cinnamon-sugar mixture.

7 Broil for 1-2 minutes on each side.

NO-FAIL MARBLE CAKE

PAREVE . YIELDS 16 SERVINGS

Our original recipe list included a "no-fail marble cake." That sounded intriguing, so we tried it. Unfortunately, it failed!! Disposing of the gloppy mess, we set out on a quest for a REAL no-fail marble cake. We found it. Easy, tasty, and truly no-fail!

6	eggs
2	cups sugar
1	cup oil
2	teaspoons vanilla extract
2	teaspoons baking powder
1½	cups cake meal
½	cup chocolate syrup

1 Preheat oven to 350°F. Lightly grease two 8" round OR 8" square pans.

2 Using an electric mixer, beat eggs with sugar until light and creamy. Gradually add oil, vanilla, baking powder, and cake meal, beating until combined. Pour ⅓ of the batter into each pan.

3 Add chocolate syrup to remaining ⅓ of the batter. Mix until smooth. Pour half of the chocolate batter into each pan and swirl gently with a knife to marbelize.

4 Bake 45-60 minutes, until toothpick inserted in center comes out clean.